Urban Communal Living

in Britain

Edited by
Penny Clark
James Dennis
Jonathan How

A Diggers & Dreamers Review

DIGGERS AND DREAMERS PUBLICATIONS

Diggers & Dreamers
Publications
2023

First published
2023
D&D Publications
BCM Edge
London
WC1N 3XX

ISBN
978-1-8384725-3-5

Distribution
Edge of Time Ltd
BCM Edge
London
WC1N 3XX
020 8133 1451

Typesetting and Layout
Jonathan How

Cover Illustration
based on artwork from
Meli Vasiloudes Bayada,
Glasgow Student Housing
Co-op

CCH

Many thank to the Confederation of Co-operative Housing for their donation towards the cost of publication.

Acknowledgements: Thank you to all our contributors and to the many communities and other organisations that have responded to our requests for information. We've also been to a couple of places for our meetings in the last two years, so grateful thanks to everyone at Braziers and Springhill.

Contents

Preface

If you mention communal living to most people the classic idea of the commune in the country might spring to mind. A big old unloved mansion occupied by unwashed adults and wild children. Traditionally 'communal living' seems to go with getting as far away as possible from 'civilisation'.

While such rural communes definitely exist (and in particular proliferated in the 1970s) many actually have their roots in urban communal living, namely the squatting movement which flourished around the same time. And although the founder members of some of those 'big house' communities moved from city to country, many of their brethren didn't. Consequently another whole branch of the communal living movement developed its own history in the towns and cities of the UK.

It's these urban communities which this book explores. It examines and gives a voice to some of the communities which have sprung up through the cracks of housing hegemony: innovating, circumnavigating, and sometimes straight-up ignoring the rules, regulations and social norms which govern housing.

In this book you will find a mixture of essays, personal accounts and how-tos, along with articles which sit somewhere in between. It was our intention to capture a snapshot of urban communal living in the UK, and to give a platform to those who have an eagle-eye view, or are in the thick of it themselves.

The "thick of it" is a good phrase to describe some of the housing movements that are explored within this book. The first article, by members of Student Co-op Homes, gives a forthright narrative of the work it's taken to establish student co-operatives in the UK. Similarly, Dr Martin Field's insightful record of UK cohousing demonstrates the different innovative methods groups have employed to bring their projects to life. A further innovative and rapidly scaling model – coliving – which is either largely unknown or mistrusted by those in communal housing circles, is examined in the article, *What is this coliving thing, anyway?* written by one of our own editors. From these contributions we can clearly see that urban communal housing is pushing the boundaries of the housing sector, both driven by and enabling rethinking on what it is we need from our homes.

This innovation – of course – comes from standing on the shoulders of giants. Blase Lambert, in his article, *Community Led Housing in the UK* narrates the history of UK housing co-operatives, and shows how the movement has been perceived as serving different purposes throughout the decades. A historical account of a very different kind, by contributor Supercrew, vividly conjures squatting in the 1960s-1970s, with his story of the rise and fall of the London Street Commune. These chapters provide slivers of insight into the rich history of communal living in the UK, something which this book nods at rather than delves into.[1]

Instead, the overriding focus is contemporary and practical. In fact, readers who are considering community living themselves may want to consult the three superb how-to/how-I-did-it articles in this book. In his article, *Urban rented communities*, communard Noah Walton makes the argument for creating an intentional community in an urban rented house-share, and gives his tried and tested framework for developing the right structures. For those who are considering cohousing, David Michael – the developer behind five cohousing communities, including the first purpose-built UK cohousing community – shares some of his knowledge and experiences of the development process. Last but not least, highly experienced co-operative member Helen Russell explores the practicalities, skills, traits and challenges associated with co-operative life, through the framework of the Seven Co-operative Principles. All three of these articles illustrate how communal living requires skills which mingle the highly practical with the social and emotional.

Not easy, one may think, but the results can be highly rewarding. This book also includes articles which focus on the experience of community life, such as the

For a more extensive historical view of communal living in the UK, see Chris Coates' *Communes Britannica*.

thoughtful and moving contribution from members of L'Arche, a community which fully embraces those with learning disabilities. Author Mim Skinner's account of the urban activist community she was part of also captures the idealism, ingenuity and intensity of opening their home to others, while fighting food waste. And homelessness activist and squatter, Michael, demystifies urban squatting through sharing his experiences of squatting in London for over a decade.

Altogether, we view these articles as capturing some of the brilliant "mess" of urban communal living, and communal living in general. This includes the potential for what might go wrong, which is explored by Ian Haworth, founder of the Cult Information Centre. His article includes an explanation of what warning signs to look out for that a community is a cult – so take note!

We're enormously grateful to the people who have contributed to this book and immensely proud of the quality of their work. We believe there is everything from nitty-gritty to national philosophical oversight. A word does need to be taken here to acknowledge what isn't in this book. This is a review of Britain, but we can hardly scratch the surface with a work of this size. There's easily a book to be written on Brighton, London or Sheffield alone. Here are just a few examples of omissions: Bristol Tiny Homes, Gannicox Camphill, Argyle Street, Blackcurrent, Brambles, Cordata, Coventry Peace House, Cornerstone, The Drive, The Nevill, Fireside, Firelight, Fruit Corner, Hargrave Road, Islington Park Street, Gifford Park, LILAC, Nutclough, On the Brink, Pendragon, Radical Routes, Rainbow, Random Camel, Rose Howey, Sanford, Share Instead, Skylark... the list goes on... from caravans lining backstreets in Glastonbury to Cornish container cul-de-sacs for the homeless... who knows, maybe next time, but for now this lot should keep you busy – enjoy!

James, Jonathan and Penny

Student Co-op Homes

LISA HARTLEY, CHRIS JARROLD, SCOTT JENNINGS AND VIVIAN WOODELL

Empowering young people to claim autonomy, work together and develop leadership skills... but are the sinks clean?

Over the last decade, a resurgence in student activism has fuelled a new movement led by students. Student Co-op Homes (SCH) was officially registered in March 2018 as a multi-stakeholder co-operative, to develop a thriving student housing co-op movement across the UK. Through direct ownership and third-party leases, SCH aims to expand its access to properties and lease onward to student housing co-operatives to manage on a day-to-day basis.

So, where did the idea of a student housing co-operative movement start in the UK?

Prior to the early 2010s several student-led co-op initiatives emerged across the UK, but they were largely fragmented with no national structures to bring them together and support them. They tended to either fizzle out or lose focus on serving students. One such example is a student housing co-operative in London in the 1970s, which ended up becoming a co-op for non-students once established.

In the mid-1990s an initiative to launch a student housing co-op movement in the UK was briefly discussed but failed to gain momentum. Other notable examples existed in the

STUDENT
CO-OP
HOMES

1970s and Manchester in 2004, all of which fizzled out over time.

With the proposed introduction of increased tuition fees and the student protests in 2010, a new generation of students were energised by the fight for affordable education. Though the protests ultimately did not succeed, a number of students across the UK were inspired to find other ways to address their economic needs in order to make their education affordable. They turned to addressing the exploitative student rental market.

In 2012 a member of an emerging Co-operative in Birmingham visited student housing co-operatives in North America. Gaining insight into how a national structure had enabled their movement to establish and grow. This visit inspired UK Student Co-operators to ask, 'why don't we have these?'.

In North America, there is a well-established and mature movement with over 4,000 students living in student housing co-operatives. The national federation for North America is known as NASCO (North American Students of Co-operation).

In 2014, student co-op groups including food, bike and re-use co-ops created Students for Co-operation (SfC), a UK-wide network of student co-ops that provided a platform for pooling resources, collaboration, and mutual aid. Around the same time several student housing co-operatives were founded and participated in the SfC network.

In February 2014, SfC held their first student co-op conference in Birmingham, with delegates from across the country putting on a whole host of valuable and in-depth workshops and networking opportunities. Further gatherings have been held since.

The first student housing co-operatives who obtained property were in Birmingham, Edinburgh, and Sheffield, with many other projects inspired to launch based on their success.

The motivation for students to establish student housing co-operatives in the UK comes from various factors relevant to different locations. In some areas, these factors relate to exploitative high rents, in others from poor quality and poorly maintained housing, and for many it is both. In 2021, The National Student Accommodation Survey found that for those who pay rent:

- Approximately 50% struggle with cost;

- Over 10% state it's a 'constant struggle';

- 60% say that their mental health is impacted by rental cost;

- Over 40% found their studying has been negatively impacted.

The Birmingham house

In 2014, Students for Co-operation obtained funding from East of England Co-operative Society to commission a report to explore how feasible it would be to create a national student housing co-operative organisation in the UK. Acorn Co-op Support conducted the study, which confirmed it was a viable proposition. A proposition that would take time to take root and begin development.

The First UK Student Housing Co-operatives / First Wave

Birmingham Student Housing Co-operative Ltd (BSHC)

In 2013, students in Birmingham saw that the co-operative model would be a solution to their poor housing situation. The existing rental

Pauline Green, President of the International Co-operative Alliance attended the opening day of Birmingham Student Housing Co-operative

Founding SEASALT members visit Birmingham, 2018

sector has poor quality, expensive housing and lacks any empowerment of students in controlling their lives. They struggled to independently obtain finance, but in 2014 The Phone Co-op, a telecoms co-operative owned and run by its customers, offered to help. The Phone Co-op bought a seven-bed property and leased it for an initial seven years. BSHC also received help from the Birmingham Co-operative Housing Services, then a part of the Accord Group and the Co-operative Enterprise Hub.

BSHC now has nine bedrooms after an expansion led by the student members. The property also features a spacious communal lounge and kitchen-diner. At the back of the house there is a large garden and evidence of this being a well loved student household with a greenhouse, workshop shed, vegetable patches, and compost bins. On Friday evenings BSHC welcomes other students and the wider community, as part of a tradition that started before the co-op was even con-ceived. These meals are an opportunity to network, socialise, talk politics, and share the freedoms of living without landlords.

Edinburgh Student Housing Co-operative (ESHC)

With 106 beds in 24 shared flats, ESHC is the largest student housing co-operative in the UK. It is the only one in the world to operate at this scale on a model of direct democracy, explicitly influenced by the ideals of anarchism. The Co-op opened in 2014, spearheaded by a small group of determined students. Without finance, experience, or a building, progress seemed unlikely. But through the support of the local authority and Castle Rock Edinvar Housing Association (CRE), a surplus block of 1990s student flats was secured on an initial five-year lease and a right for ESHC to buy the property at any time. CRE also agreed for the lease and associated legal fees to be paid in arrears by ESHC.

Before and After photos of basement conversion

The lease provides ESHC with the ability to rework the fabric of their building to suit co-operative living. The most prominent example of this has been the conversion of former basement spaces used for car parking and storage, into new communal spaces.

This conversion project was student-led and to the specification of the Co-operative, taking several years to complete. Much of the work was undertaken by the residents themselves as part of a paid work programme to reimburse members for their input. This project introduced two common areas into their buildings, new washing facilities, a new office space/server area and a much-improved external garden / bike storage area for members to enjoy. The resourcefulness of students, when given the opportunity and autonomy, is evident from this project.

Sheffield Student Housing Co-operative (SSHC)

In 2015, SSHC opened its doors with a 5-bed property. What had started as a dissertation project in 2012 took three years to become a reality. Like Birmingham, the group couldn't obtain finance independently and so worked with The Phone Co-op who purchased the property and leased it to SSHC.

SSHC by the time it had property had undergone changes as a group of students with founder members having already / about to graduate and moved away – a common occurrence for student housing co-operatives. North West Housing Services was appointed to provide services supporting finances and property management, although the co-op has full control and autonomy over spending decisions.

Nottingham Student Housing Co-operative (NSHC)

The Nottingham Student Housing Co-operative was founded in early 2015. Inspired by the launches of other student housing co-ops they were motivated to action by poor housing standards affecting students' physical and mental health and a desire for student led housing that would put them in control now and in the future.

Many of the students involved were heavily engaged in student activism / student union politics and felt that their university had washed their hands of a housing situation they had a hand in creating, detrimental to both students and the wider community. The students were determined to prove the issue was not students, but the existing private rental sector which did not serve the interests of students.

Nottingham Student Housing Co-operative
Buck the landlords

Much like Birmingham and Sheffield, they struggled to obtain independent finance, they approached larger Co-operatives in their local area and The Phone Co-op. They found that the former were keen to see the progress the first student housing co-operatives would make, and The Phone Co-op had already spent a considerable amount of capital to support BSHC and SSHC.

NSHC members strategically focused on developing what would become SCH, they saw it as the best opportunity to acquire property not just for themselves, but for other student housing co-operatives across the UK.

Glasgow Student Housing Co-operative (GSHC)

The founding members of Glasgow (GSHC) were originally inspired by a visit to ESHC. GSHC was set up in 2016 and while they have secured some funding towards their development, they are still in the process of securing a property.

GSHC set up in direct response to the frustration that inexperienced students, with an overall lack of understanding of their rights in housing are exploited and live with little control over their living situations.

They believe that a housing co-op is an effective way to combat increasing rent prices and provide a democratic living environment with students in control of their housing. They are excited to set up a housing co-operative which allows students to have more rights and freedoms such as owning pets, the right to decorate and make larger changes to their property around accessibility and sustainability agendas.

Collage craft night hosted by Glasgow Student Housing Co-op

Momentum Builds

In 2017 the proposal for a national organisation to develop the UK Student Housing Co-operative Movement was pitched at Co-operatives Congress. Inspired by prior interactions with North American Student Housing Co-operatives (NASCO) and the desire to develop a new generation of Co-operators, Co-operatives UK agreed to support development of the organisation.

In March 2018, Student Co-operative Homes officially registered as a multi-stakeholder co-operative. This enabled student co-ops and supporters to come together to build a national organisation, raise finance and create a stable infrastructure to grow the movement.

SCH received generous support from Co-operatives UK, Mid-Counties Co-operative, East of England Co-operative and The Phone Co-op Foundation for Co-operative Innovation, and Radical Routes. The contributions and services offered enabled the creation of branding and marketing materials, the writing of bespoke primary rules and crucially the employment of SCH's first part-time project worker. This enabled SCH to excel at a time of lower student capacity and engagement, due to how long the idea and organisation took to develop.

A transatlantic solidarity agreement was signed between NASCO and SCH in the same year that led to the beginning of collaborations, knowledge exchange and mutual visits between the organisations, such as SCH representation at the NASCO Institute and both organisations jointly affiliating to Co-operative Housing International (CHI) subsequently.

In 2019, Student Co-op Homes launched its first Community Share Offer and raised £300k for acquisition of property. In 2020 a new part-time Operations Manager was employed as development of the society was transferred from Co-operatives UK to SCH.

Around a similar time to the founding of SCH, SEASALT Housing Co-operative in Brighton also began organising (see case study at the end). In 2021, SCH purchased its first property in Nottingham.

In September 2022 several UK and Irish student housing co-ops and SCH board members attended an event hosted by Co-operative Housing International in Switzerland to plan, alongside student housing co-ops from other European countries, how to build pan-European collaboration for mutual benefit. This may lead to an association similar to NASCO being developed in Europe.

As of January 2023 we have active member co-ops in Birmingham, Brighton (SEASALT), Belfast, Bristol, Cork (Ireland), Edinburgh, Glasgow, Nottingham, Manchester (MASH) and Sheffield.

There are also other projects independent of SCH membership who are interested in collaborations and in regular contact with SCH.

Map of current Student Co-op Homes members

It is worth mentioning in the last decade there have also been nascent groups in Leeds, Norwich (NACHOS), Stirling and Exeter.

The Challenges of Our Ambitions:

It wasn't always easy. At times student engagement flagged as some things have taken longer than expected, there were occasional tensions around the vision for the organisation, how

its democracy would function, and expectations members had of it. Given the natural turnover of the student population, it's important to work hard on maintaining engagement and keeping the vision alive.

One of the most notable debates in SCH's development was whether to have a board of directors or a general meeting of delegates as its governance model. It was eventually decided to go with the option that would be most familiar and appealing to Investor-Supporter Members and other funders, which was to have an identifiable group of people that were taking formal responsibility for the organisation and give representation to Investor-Supporter Members in day-to-day decision making. This led to SCH adopting a board structure.

SCH is currently working out how to enable more participation and skill sharing across its network and how to access external training. This aim is to enable pooling of existing skills and resources, facilitate mutual aid, and ensure the movement is well educated beyond basic co-operative skills. Under this general theme of education is the desire to provide students with the co-operative organisational skills and the knowledge to become empowered and skilful in taking control of their housing situation. A further positive outcome was that it also served as a pathway into the co-op movement and several students have gone on to work in, or become active members of consumer or workers co-ops, as well as live in other housing co-ops as graduates.

After the share issue closed in March 2020, we planned to start the property search and purchase our first SCH owned property. However, Covid-related challenges made it difficult for us to proceed, the housing market was frozen by the government for a period and travel restrictions made property visits and surveys very difficult to arrange. There was also uncertainty about whether students would return to campus in September 2020 due to the pandemic.

Eventually, in January 2021 we were able to acquire our first property, in Nottingham. By this time the market had become very "hot" due to the national stamp duty holiday and pent-up demand. We were gazumped more than once.

Sadly, after some months passed, SCH became aware of local interpretations of regulations by Broxtowe Borough Council that meant this property was non-compliant with minimum room size. The room itself met national minimum requirements, but this local rule was more stringent, meaning only four lettable rooms available of the expected five. There were existing aspirational plans to convert the loft to make a possible seven-bedroom configuration. Options were explored to make the smallest room bigger, as well as exploring the proposed loft conversion, but unfortunately these were not feasible at that time.

The SCH board reviewed the situation with NSHC and concluded there was no practical option but to sell the property. A small surplus was made on the sale of the property.

Following the decision to sell the Nottingham property, SCH reflected on its processes and best practice and has undertaken a review of its property acquisition strategy, scoping exercises of local legislation, documentation of best practice, and development of more training opportunities for directors.

As part of this review, the Society established more stringent pre-lease and ongoing lease responsibilities. This includes policy requirements and what the co-ops can expect from SCH by way of support to meet these requirements.

Where are we now?

With the sale of the property in Nottingham and investments / loan financing coming via various partnerships we are actively seeking to acquire properties across the UK for our student housing co-op members.

We are working on the transfer of the Birmingham and Sheffield properties, originally purchased by The Phone Co-op and leased to their local student housing co–ops, from The Midcounties Co–operative which acquired them when The Phone Co-op merged with Midcounties. Midcounties is supporting this transaction by investing share capital in Student Co-operative Homes thus becoming partners in the project.

Case Study:
SEASALT Housing Co-operative

SEASALT (South East Students Autonomously Living Together) was founded in early 2018 following student union elections at The University of Sussex and feasibility discussions in Brighton. Their goal was to create affordable, high-quality housing for students run by students. A core working group of students from the University of Brighton and the University of Sussex was formed.

With skyrocketing rents, the idea of a student housing co-op started nearly a decade earlier. It featured on the manifesto of at least two previous sabbatical officers. However, it wasn't until 2018, when the Brighton and Hove Community Land Trust (BHCLT) launched its grant programme, that the housing co-op applied for funding and secured a part-time community-led housing enabler.

With support from BHCLT, a grant application was made to Homes England. To secure the £40k grant, SEASALT needed to raise £10k of match funding. After several meetings, a £10k donation was received from the University of Sussex, making it the first University to donate to a student housing co-op. SEASALT also secured funding from Reach, to help them become "investment ready". SEASALT was in a very fortunate financial position but spent considerable time and energy trying to meet funding spend requirements.

Over the next 3.5 years, the group attended training sessions run by BHCLT, promoted, and raised awareness at events, and developed a strong reputation locally. They looked at various large properties, which would be ideal for a co-op. It was agreed very early on not to consider smaller family homes, already a source of contention locally as landlords were evicting local families and turning them into Houses of Multiple Occupation (HMOs).

SEASALT carried out extensive door-knocking campaigns, a critical step to building up support in the local community. On the streets, the students conducted an effective listening campaign that turned the community around, challenging initial assumptions about loud partying students. Following the door knocking campaign,

SEASALT received thirty-one letters of support and only four objections to a planning application for a large property which they were unsuccessful in obtaining. An amazing achievement.

Door knocking listening campaign

It was hard to come by suitable properties, and the challenge of how to raise enough money for a deposit in one of the most expensive cities in the UK still loomed.

Luckily all their work didn't go unnoticed, as BHCLT proposed that through their community share offer, they could purchase a property and lease it directly to SEASALT.

Throughout the partnership with BHCLT, SEASALT regularly reviewed the relationship, focusing on communication to ensure that it remained student-led and SEASALT remained involved in decision making on the properties. Initially, BHCLTs planned to raise share capital for multiple projects in the city. However, when covid struck, this was revised,

and they decided to concentrate their fundraising efforts on SEASALT alone.

SEASALT members played a crucial role in the fundraising for the BHCLT share offer. The students used their networks, making links with lecturers, the University, and parents. With a successful share offer under their belt, BHCLT progressed a property search and found a suitable property, with seven students moving into the property in September 2021.

The co-op house has a large back garden (especially by Brighton standards) and a small front garden. SEASALT wants to landscape the back-garden with their tenant's involvement and has developed a plan to improve accessibility of the property over several stages.

SEASALT has also undertaken work with Brighton and Hove Energy Services Co-op (BHESCo), and Warmer Sussex to complete an energy audit of the house. Providing a comprehensive overview of the measures and improvements they could adopt to reduce energy loss and make the house greener.

SEASALT have always been keen to raise awareness about student housing co-operatives and have presented at various events across the UK, including at Stir to Action's 'Playground for the New Economy' festival, York Design week, and The World Transformed and Reclaim Pride. They were scouted by Paul Kelly, the director of Breaking Ground Liverpool, a community-led housing festival for the Liverpool city region. Following the event, City councillors stayed in contact with SEASALT members and now want to set up a housing co-op of their own as part of CLH developments resulting from the Metro Mayors land commission – the first of its kind in the UK.

By the time this article goes to print Student Co-op Homes expects to be negotiating loan finance and share capital investments from Scotmid to support acquisition of property in Glasgow.

What Student Co-operators have done after Housing Co-ops

Here are just a few other examples of what founding members and former residents have gone on to set up or got involved in.

Some are in co-operatives such as worker co-ops like the Birmingham Bike Foundry, and consumer co-ops i.e. The Phone Co-op/ MidCounties Co-op.

Some have gone on into roles in representational organisations / national federations such as the Confederation of Co-operative Housing (CCH) and Co-operative Housing International (CHI).

Many have co-created new co-operatives such as The Warehouse Cafe and Stirchley Co-op Development.

A number have moved on to live in and/or participate in the Radical Routes network and their housing co-ops such as Cornerstone, Gung Ho, Dragonfly, Out of Town, and Bruadair.

One has changed the direction of their work and taken a PhD in researching worker co-operatives internationally.

Glasgow students visit ESHC, 2022

Students for Co-operation Gatherings

Events and networking opportunities have played a fundamental role in the development of the student co-operator network.

In February 2014, SfC held its first student co-op conference in Birmingham, with delegates from across the country putting on a whole host of valuable and in-depth workshops and networking opportunities. This included a talk from NASCO on how to build a co-operative federation.

Gatherings like this happened between 2014-2019 and are vital to building awareness of wider co-operation as well as raising awareness and developing community organising skills amongst students.

In 2022, SfC hosted its first in-person gathering in three years at ESHC, with students from across the UK. There were opportunities for networking, communal meals, drinks, a dance party, plus ESHC's debut play called "Eat The Rich!", A satirical comedy about class, hippies, vegans, and vampires.

In only a few years, students across the UK have achieved a lot. Student Co-op Homes can't wait to welcome in more members and continue to grow a thriving student housing co-op network.

How you could help

SCH is excited to be at the forefront of this movement. We know this model works and lasts for the long term. We know it improves people's experience of their education and introduces people to co-operation at a formative time in their lives. SCH is always looking to new opportunities, new cities, and partners to collaborate with to increase the number of beds available to students to give them that Co-operative option and challenge a broken housing market that doesn't serve student interests.

We are open to communications and building new links and relationships – please get in touch, we are interested in hearing from:

- Housing Associations

- Local/Regional Government

- Community Land Trusts

- Co-operatives

- Students' Unions

- Universities

- Student networks

Together we can create the kind of student living that we all want and help to generate new co-operators now and into the future.

For more information on Student Co-op Homes see

Web: **www.studenthomes.coop**

Facebook: **facebook.com/NoMoreLandlords**

Twitter: **twitter.com/NoMoreLandlords**

Linktree: **linktr.ee/studentcoophomes**

Bibliography

- M. Shaw and S. Farmelo, 'Co-operatives: Resisting the Housing Crisis', in Resist!: Against a Precarious Future, R. Filar, Ed. London: Lawrence & Wishart, 2015. A look at the housing crisis and the establishment of Edinburgh Student Housing Co-operative.

- H. Kallin and M. Shaw, 'Escaping the Parasite of the Student Flat: Reflections on an experiment in co-operative housing', Radical Housing Journal, vol. 1, no. 1, pp. 223–226, 2019. Article on Edinburgh Student Housing Co-operative as well as the demonisation of students in Edinburgh.

- L. Kelly, 'Student co-operative pioneers a reduction in university housing costs', The Guardian, March 13, 2013. Article on the establishment of Birmingham Student Housing Co-operative.

- S. Farmelo, 'Student co-operatives fight back against exploitative landlords', The Guardian, May 03, 2013. An overview of the establishment of SfC and Birmingham Student Housing Co-operative.

- S. Farmelo and H. Craig, 'The Housing Crisis: Co-operative Alternatives', Stir, Summer 2013 Article on the establishment of Birmingham Student Housing Co-operative and Students for Co-operation.

- R. Colvin, 'How young people, technology and co-op values are creating a better future', The Guardian, March 26, 2014. An account of the 2014 founding conference of Students for Co-operation.

- S. Bradley, 'Tired of your landlord? A student co-operative could be the answer', The Guardian, April 30, 2014. Article on student housing co-ops.

- M. Allen, 'Birmingham Students Housing Co-op on a solution to exploitative landlords', The Guardian, July 25, 2014. Article on the establishment of Birmingham Student Housing Co-operative.

- N. Seth-Smith, 'Students, why not be your own landlord?', New Internationalist, September 04, 2014. Article on the establishment of Edinburgh Student Housing Co-operative with interviews of members.

- A. Voinea, 'Students for Co-operation conference: a tour of Edinburgh co-ops', Co-op News, November 18, 2014. An account from the 2014 SfC Edinburgh conference.

- E. Lunn, 'Student co-ops open their doors to tackle sky-high accommodation costs', The Observer, September 07, 2015. Article on the opening of Sheffield Student Housing Co-operative alternative student housing providers.

- A. Bounds, 'New co-operatives aim to cut cost of student accommodation', Financial Times, March 20, 2018. About the 2018 launch of the Student Co-op Homes share offer.

- M. Hadfield, 'Heart of England society invests £100k in student housing co-ops', Co-op News, January 31, 2020. About the Student Co-op Homes share issue.

Lisa Hartley
is the Operations Manager for Student Co-op Homes, which is a member-led co-operative aiming to build a thriving and large scale student housing co-operative movement. She has been working with student co-operatives for over five years, and was instrumental in setting up SEASALT Housing Co-operative.

Chris Jarrold
is a User Director for Student Co-op Homes. He lived in BSHC for over two years and has been involved with SCH as a director since day one. He also contributes to Radical Routes and Workers' Co-ops.

Scott Jennings
is an NHS Doctor and founded Nottingham Student Housing Co-op. He was Project Manager during creation of SCH, and acts as Vice Chair. He's also a Director of the Confederation of Co-operative Housing and Co-operative Housing International.

Vivian Woodell
has been supporting the student housing co-operative sector since its inception, and as well as being a board member of Student Co-op Homes, has various other co-op roles including CEO of The Phone Co-op Foundation for Co-operative Innovation, Vice President of The Midcounties Co-operative Ltd., Vice President of Co-operatives Europe, and director of The Co-operative Loan Fund and West Oxfordshire Community Transport Limited.

Community Led Housing in the UK

BLASE LAMBERT

Confederation of Co-operative Housing CEO Blase Lambert describes co-operative history in terms of three phases, demonstrating the legacy of the co-operative movement on community-led housing today.

A Slow Start

The early foundations for communities owning and managing their homes in formal collective models were laid when Robert Owen took over the management of David Dale's cotton mills in Lanark in 1800 and, after breaking with his partners, his creation of the New Lanark model community. He established the New Lanark Village Store which was run by and for the benefit of the community in 1813 and is held to be the father of socialism and the co-operative movement; New Lanark is a UNESCO World Heritage Site.

The co-operative legal form was further developed by William Thompson in his publication 'An Inquiry into the Principles of the Distribution of Wealth' in 1824 and by Dr William King who set up a co-operative store in Brighton and created the 'The Co-operator' periodical in 1828.

The Rochdale Pioneers established what is held to be the world's first co-operative in 1844 and their Rule Book stated an objective of their newly formed society as "the building of a number of homes in which those members desiring to assist each other in improving their domestic and social conditions may reside".

However, unlike in Austria and Germany, the housing co-operative model did not take hold during the nineteenth century in the UK and by the turn of the century, with the exception of the creation of garden cities by Ebezener Howard and others, little changed as community led housing approaches made a slow start.

Academics and supporters of the community led housing sector often point to countries like Norway and Sweden, where significant proportions of homes are developed by housing co-operatives, but the picture in these countries was made possible because of post-war public housing policies introduced there. In the UK, public policy was focused on public sector housebuilding with successive governments during the 1950s and 1960s boasting of having built more council homes than their rival parties.

The First Wave of Community Led Housing – Housing Co-operatives

It is not until 1974 that community led housing would benefit from dedicated government policy. The Housing Minister at that time, Reg Freeson MP, launched a policy that would see 450 housing co-operatives set up in England. These ownership housing co-operatives were the first wave of community led housing; they rented homes to members primarily on low incomes in urban areas and their development was supported by the creation of a network of secondary co-operatives and the National Federation of Housing Co-operatives; at the same time 47 housing co-operatives were set up in Scotland.

During this first wave, a significant number of housing co-operatives were also created without government funding; such as the short-life movement where co-operatives were formed to take on management of empty homes and ownership co-operatives were developed using loanstock and bank finance pioneered by Radical Routes.

Government policy throughout the 1980s moved firmly toward individual home ownership and focused social housing development on a reducing number of large housing associations. An overdependence on dwindling governmental financial support and poor governance during the 1980s led to the bankruptcy of the National Federation of Housing Co-operatives in 1990, a decline in the number of housing co-operatives to 220 in England and 19 in Scotland and the end of development by secondary co-operatives.

The first wave had created many co-operatives that have sustained, but the 20,000 homes owned and managed by them demonstrates that the community led housing sector had failed to seize a significant part of the housing market during this first wave.

The Second Wave of Community Led Housing – An Alternative for Council Housing

The second wave of community led housing came about as support for council housing as it began to wane. Communities began choosing to manage their own estates and the growth in tenant management co-operatives on urban council housing estates throughout the 1980s. This led to Right to Manage legislation for local authority tenants in 1994; to date there are 250 tenant management organisations (TMOs) that are managing 75,000 tenanted and leasehold homes.

The Major and Blair governments accelerated the sale of council housing beyond the individual ownership model of the Thatcher government's Right to Buy with stock transfer programmes which saw large numbers of council homes sold to housing associations. The 1992 transfer of 921 homes by Westminster City Council to Walterton and Elgin Community Homes is an early forerunner of the community led alternatives which would follow.

The Confederation of Co-operative Housing, which had been set up in 1994 as a successor to the National Federation of Housing Co-operatives, sought to create a community led stock transfer model and developed the Community Gateway Model. The first resident owned stock transfer was created in Preston in 2005 with the transfer of 6,153 homes and a further 7 such transfers of council housing in England and Wales have seen 50,000 homes move into community ownership.

The first stock transfer of a TMO group took place in Walsall with the establishment of WATMOS in 2002 and in 2012 Rochdale Boroughwide Homes was created which is the first jointly owned resident and employee stock transfer; these transfers added a further 15,000 homes. The second wave had seen community led approaches applied to providing an alternative for council housing but the 135,000 homes that came under community ownership and management represented a small part of the massive shift of ownership that was made away from council housing to housing associations during the 1990s and 2000s.

Confederation of Co-operative Housing

In 1992, a group of 'Concerned Co-operators' came together to create a new voice for the housing co-operative sector. This group of co-operators incorporated the Confederation of Co-operative Housing (CCH) in 1994; since then it has been the representative organisation for housing co-operatives in the UK and a federal member of Co-operatives UK.

CCH exists to promote viable forms of co-operative, mutual and community led housing. It assists its members in enhancing their governance, delivering excellent services and in planning for the future as well as providing networking and learning opportunities through its annual conference, member forums and training programmes.

CCH is committed to working with its partners in the UK. It has a long established partnership with the national tenant organisations (NFTMO, TAROE and TPAS) and more recently it was a founding member of Community Led Homes (with CLT Network, Locality and UK Cohousing Network). It is also committed to working internationally and its Chief Officer is a Board member of the International Co-operative Alliance (ICA) and is the Treasurer of Co-operative Housing International (the ICA global housing sector body).

Centre of Excellence

CCH provides advice and support to its members and to groups starting up co-operative and other community led housing organisations; it has developed this service over a 25 year period to include:

Publication of the Codes of Governance for Housing Co-operatives and Community Led Housing Organisations;

Publication of subsidiary guidance including Governance and Management, Financial Planning, Active Membership, Complaints Handling and Achieving and Measuring Value for Money;

Maintenance of a substantial database of model policies and procedures;

Publication of model rules for general meeting governed housing co-operatives, leaseholder land co-operatives, mutual home ownership societies, Registered Provider housing co-operatives and tenant management co-operatives;

Delivery of training and accreditation programmes for housing co-operatives and community led housing advisors;

Delivery of bespoke advice and support services including climate change and retrofitting, organisational health checks, conflict

resolution, policy and rules reviews, performance management, membership and involvement, business planning, financial control and management, leadership and development;

Creation of the Wayshaper options planning tool and associated resources for advisors working with new community led housing organisations and, currently in development, the Wayshaper Sustainable Development Goals planning tool.

CCH Membership

CCH promotes the excellent work done by co-operative and other community led housing organisations. We foster communication between our members and serve the sector, campaigning for quality co-operative and community led solutions to meet the housing needs of communities across the United Kingdom.

Becoming a CCH member:

• makes you part of our growing and thriving movement for change and community – housing co-operatives, tenant management organisations, cohousing societies, mutual home ownership societies and other community led housing organisations that are about people and communities developing their own housing solutions;

• brings you into the global co-operative movement – it is estimated that more than one billion people are members of co-operatives and two billion people use their services;

• enables you to shape the UK – co-operative and community led housing sector of the future – CCH is a major community led housing sector stakeholder and our membership's views matter;

• gives you access to our member services – helping co-operative and community led housing organisations to become and remain strong and sustainable and meet their day-to-day challenges.

For further information visit the CCH website at www.cch.coop

**The Third Wave of Community Led Housing
– Homes for All**

The first two waves of community led housing were restricted to social and low cost housing which is unlike the picture in many other countries. In the UK, we do not restrict access to co-operative retailers, insurance providers or funeral services on the basis of income. Community led housing options and solutions are not just for the poorest in our society or a final role of the dice when public sector services have hit hard times; they are for everyone.

Since 2011 government programmes have seen a re-energising of community led housing development through the £100m Empty Homes programme (2011-15) in England, the Welsh Government co-operative housing programme (since 2012) and the £250m Community Housing Fund programme (since 2016) in England; government support is also emerging in Scotland.

It is within a broader view that community led housing is for everyone that people have begun to innovate and create the models that are right for their needs. Whether it is students that don't want to be exploited by the financialisaton of halls of residence, young people who want an alternative to unaffordable home ownership or overpriced private renting, groups of older people who want an alternative to a traditional care home, multi-generational groups that want to live in a mutually supportive environment or people who want to create a better and more sustainable future; the emergence of community land trusts, cohousing communities, mutual home ownership societies, student housing co-operatives and new forms of collective ownership are presenting the possibility that the third wave will be the decisive wave. It is with this hope for the future that I have penned this contribution to this timely review of the urban landscape of communal and co-operative solutions to the lived experience in the UK.

Blase Lambert
is the Chief Officer of the Confederation of Co-operative Housing, Treasurer of Co-operative Housing International, and Board Member of the International Co-operative Alliance.

The Co-operative Principles

HELEN RUSSELL

In this article Two Piers Housing Co-op veteran Helen uses the Seven Co-operative Principles to explore what participating in a co-operative enterprise means. Spoiler alert: filing is important.

Co-operativism is a dynamic, evolutionary and a consistent aspiration to be co-operative, and the central themes of co-operation are democracy and member participation. Following the Co-operative Principles promotes a particular kind of participation in a housing co-op, because of the peculiarity of being member, tenant and landlord all at the same time. How might members in an ownership co-op bring about a meaningful expression of the idea of participation? An interesting archaic use of the verb 'to participate' is 'to receive a part or share of'. It's from the Latin and breaks down into *capere* meaning 'to take', and *pars,* meaning 'a part'. Not only does this word mean to take part *in* something, but it means to take a part *of* something. This means that living in a housing co-operative is about both having and giving – having a secure home among friends, and giving back to the community some mutually beneficial contribution. It also means that a high degree of commitment is necessary to make it work.

This essay is primarily about the Co-operative Principles, which I began to consider in some depth as a prelude to training other co-operators in their art. I suggest that the seven Co-operative Principles can be put into three groups, or three commitments: equality, unity and security. These are the commitments which co-operativism makes to us, and which we in

turn make to each other, with each principle having
an underlying attitude or practice.

PRINCIPLE	PRACTICE
First Commitment: Equality	
1: Open membership	compromise
2: Equal voting rights	democracy
3: Equal economic input	shared equity
Second Commitment: Unity	
4: Autonomy	collective identity
5: Education	belonging through understanding
Third Commitment: Security	
6: Co-operation between co-operatives	collaboration
7: Concern for Community	sustainable development

There is a progression through the principles which
describes a circular evolutionary process. This develops from the concept of open membership through
to the growth of a caring community, which in turn
will evolve a greater tolerance of difference, a more
democratic way of life, and a deeper sense that caring
for each other brings, in return, care for oneself. It is
in this co-operative context that people can genuinely
participate in a collective enterprise, and make it work.

The Three Commitments

Co-operative participation is founded in a commitment
to equality. The first three co-operative principles (open
membership, equal voting rights, and equal economic
input) are at the core of co-operative life. In terms of
who can be members, *how* they organise and conduct
themselves, and *what* they are organised to achieve,
they express the underlying value of equality.

Commitment 1 – Equality

**First Co-operative Principle of voluntary and
open membership**

*"Co-operatives are voluntary organisations, open to all persons able to use
their services and willing to accept the responsibilities of membership, without
gender, social, racial, political or religious discrimination"*

Co-operative participation depends on evolving a group identity based on respect for and tolerance of difference. Thus, the first attitude of co-operation is compromise. Positive reactions to the idea of compromise involve: finding a middle course, making mutual concessions, give and take, bargaining, reconciliation, settlement or truce, negotiation, and understanding. However, negative responses can be a fear of jeopardy, risk, ensuing discredit, and yielding up or relinquishing one's stake.

The importance of compromise for co-operators is that decisions can be made collectively through reaching consensus. *The group is strengthened through its ability to be flexible.*

Not surprisingly co-operative compromise is tricky for most of us to do. We are brought up in a culture which is predominantly interested in the development of the individual, and which has allowed, and indeed encouraged, an erosion of community values. Attempts to rediscover and re-establish the principles of co-operation are going to be hampered by an internalised resistance to those principles. How can this resistance be countered? Through a commitment to the consistent re-education of the members, at all levels. No one is immune to their conditioning. If you really want your co-op to achieve a high level of participation, there must be in place the mechanisms which enable all the members to reach agreement as to the aims and objectives of the co-op, and also the willingness to work towards achieving those aims.

Second Co-operative Principle of democratic member control and equal voting rights

"Co-operatives are democratic organisations controlled by their members, who actively participate in setting their policies and making decisions. Men and women serving as elected representatives are accountable to the membership. In primary co-operatives, members have equal voting rights (one member, one vote) and co-operatives at other levels are also organised in a democratic manner."

What does the word "democracy" mean to us? Democracy can be defined as "a form of government in which the supreme power is vested in the people collectively; a state of society characterised by recognition of equality of rights and privileges". Matters, including representation, the interpretation of constitutional matters, and the co-op's rules and procedures, are raised when we consider democracy in the co-operative context. Sanction, authority and authorisation are concerns for us as we evolve during our lives as co-operators. These are issues not only on account of their practical appearance in the everyday running of the co-op, but because so much of our humanity is touched – and triggered – by them.

An individual's sense of their own power, in terms of their ability and feeling of authority, is confronted in a co-op, or indeed any organisation which collectively undertakes a task over time and with changing circumstances. Achieving democracy in any group, be it a co-op or a nation, depends on the recognition and understanding of the mechanisms of power. It is beyond the scope of this essay to go into this too deeply. However, one basic issue can be considered: there is democracy in theory and democracy in practice. It's one thing to believe in equality of rights and privileges, but often quite another to live by that belief in everyday life. This is because everyone has their own particular psychological makeup, and their own life experience which informs everything they think and do. A person's sense of power develops from this, and it will be different in every case.

Not everyone is willing or equipped to take the initiative, solve problems, or go campaigning. But everyone without doubt has something to offer. Therefore we should not get hung up on the roles members play. Some will want to be the chair, the secretary, etc., others will want to mind the kids during meetings. *The key to democracy in a co-op is to see every contribution as an act of responsibility.* Every member will feel validated and part of things. When problems need to be solved, no doubt the solutions will be generated by the people who have familiarity with the issues. However, democracy in practice means ensuring that the decision making process is accessible to everyone. The babysitter's and the window cleaner's vote is as essential as the treasurer's – essential because without it, the co-op will degenerate into an elitist hierarchy.

Co-operative member participation requires a democratic management structure which is designed to enable the members to take on as much control of their affairs as they decide, and which can accommodate different views and attitudes. Each individual member must decide what they can contribute, and what level of control they personally feel comfortable with. The co-op's game plan must reflect this in the extent to which it collectively takes control of its affairs. At one end of the spectrum, every member might be a hardcore activist. This will produce a co-op which runs itself with a vengeance! At the other end, members may be lost in their own worlds. This co-op will hand over management lock, stock and barrel to an agency.

Co-ops are microcosms of society and psychological types — but a co-operative is a joint enterprise in which the several types have agreed to work together. Democratic control means collective control by the membership. Whatever their type, everyone's role in the collective is important. Democratic control means that each member is accountable to every other member, and it means that the members are dependent on each other. This is not the same as the dependency culture that goes along with giving management responsibility away to the experts. It is dependency founded in mutual respect for the other person's ability to contribute in their own way.

Collective democracy is about equals managing each other. There may well be no harder path for a bunch of individuals to follow! But the true basis of success for a co-operative enterprise is a shared commitment among its members to the achievement of genuine democracy, genuine equality. Such a sense of commitment can only arise when the joint nature of the enterprise and its value are fully understood by the members. In practice, for instance, this might mean accepting majority decision. But it also means debate, lobbying, holding on to one's opinions and trying to persuade others to one's viewpoint. All this talking is an exciting part of co-op life. Communication between members about everyday matters or the Co-op's long-term goals is fundamental to participation. How can members get involved if they don't know what's going on? How can they understand if they don't hear co-op-speak around them? Without the persistent exchange of ideas, the "supreme power" cannot be exercised collectively.

In the actual life of a co-op members come and go, and there's a mix of short and long term members. Change is inevitable and needs to be welcomed as an opportunity for re-evaluation. In practice, member turnover means that there will always be some members who know more, and others who know less. For a co-op not to be undermined by this fact of life, a very careful watch must be kept for any hierarchical development.

It's very easy and indeed can seem to be the expedient thing to do to allow the same old hacks who have always done things to keep their old jobs. This is bad for them – they get bored, start feeling over-worked, wonder where their lives have gone, and the quality of their contribution can suffer. It's bad for new members too. They need the opportunity to test themselves, and even if it's frustrating for the old members to suffer their inevitable mistakes, it's essential to allow them to try.

Keeping watch is as much the responsibility of new members as of old members, but old members have twice the responsibility – to watch out for the new members being able to keep an eye on them! This strange circularity, where everyone attempts to watch out for everyone else's equality, whatever their level, is fundamental to a co-op's success: success is not necessarily measured only in concrete terms, but in terms of how peacefully and creatively people can live together. If abstract co-operation is achieved, the concrete will follow by itself!

Therefore, to achieve a fully democratic co-operative, the most important activity for older members is to promote co-operative values and principles to the new members. Don't ever forget that any kind of co-operative undertaking pits itself against the opposite principles of hierarchy, exploitation, and inequality. These are almost innate and it requires collective stamina and an underlying stability to counter them. Co-operative life is visionary life, and co-operators must be proud of their undertaking, and enthusiastic about its success. Participation only becomes a problem when this sense of vision and pride is lost in the day to day practical running of a co-op.

Putting equalities at the heart of all policy

Over and above the written Equalities Policy, a co-op needs to develop an internalised sense of equality. Co-op members need to learn to filter all their co-op activities through 'Equality Spectacles'. There are differences in ability, aspirations, availability and attitudes for starters. None of these matter however, if account is taken of them. That sounds contradic-tory but it isn't! By becoming mutually aware of difference – because everyone is different after all – people feel respected by each other, and so their differences cease to separate them. Instead difference joins people together.

So, a co-op can succeed and achieve a high level of participation even with all this difference. A management structure can be worked out so that almost everyone has a job to do. Jobs in co-op management cover a huge range of ability, and all co-op members can aspire to the heights of running their own co-op.

Third Co-operative Principle of Equal Economic Contribution

"Members contribute equitably to, and democratically control, the capital of their co-operative. At least part of that capital is usually the common property of the co-operative. Members usually receive limited compensation, if any, on capital subscribed as a condition of membership. Members allocate surpluses for any or all of the following purposes: developing their co-operative, possibly by setting up reserves, part of which at least would be indivisible; benefiting members in proportion to their transactions with the co-operative; and supporting other activities approved by the membership."

The third principle of co-operation is shared equity – or common property. The idea of shared equity – in a co-op – involves impartial allocation and fair division. It can also generate the negative attitude of "I do more, I deserve more".

A housing co-op is a business. A medium sized co-op developed in the 1980s has an annual rental income of around £200,000. This can be attached to assets of around £10m, taking into account renovated and new build stock. The business of the co-op is to ensure that rents come in, bills get paid, small surpluses gradually accumulate and are apportioned. This is all very abstract, however. How does the fact that the co-op is a business affect the daily life of members? And in a housing co-op, does the principle of equity touch other areas?

There are three basic areas in which equity is a governing principle:

i) What do members contribute?

The first of these questions is two-fold. Members pay rent, but they also contribute in terms of time spent doing things for the co-op. It's very important that both of these are understood as payment to the co-operative. In many co-ops, it is only because members contribute their time and energy that the rents can be kept at affordable levels. In co-ops which employ staff, members' contributions in terms of input at meetings and work parties are essential so that staff can be properly instructed. Participatory contributions must be seen by the members to be fairly shared out, or resentment will appear and the co-op as a whole will suffer.

The rent issue can seem complicated, but application of the principle of equal economic contribution can simplify matters. There are three aspects of equality which need to be reflected in a co-operative rent policy. The first is parity. This will need to be addressed if a co-op has some tenants on pre-1998 Fair Rents and some holding tenancies granted after that date. Post-1988 re-let rents are under the jurisdiction of the landlord, and can be set at whatever level is deemed appropriate. Private landlords will on the whole take full advantage of their release from rent control. However, a housing co-op is only concerned with covering its costs and ensuring that it stays in the black. The point is that because the properties are owned in common by the membership, no individual member or group of members should be made responsible for an unequal share of expenditure. That is, their rental input should be 'the same'. Secondly, rent levels should be consistent with each other, and thirdly, any differentials on account of size, amenities, and original costs, if recognised, must be seen to be fair.

ii) What do they receive as individual members?

Individual members can expect to receive the full benefits of living in a housing co-op. These are both practical and personal. In a fully mutual, their tenancy is safe and sound so long as they pay their rent and get involved in running the Co-op. They can expect their accommodation to be developed and maintained to a good standard, as long as they ensure that repairs get carried out, and they run their maintenance budgets carefully. They can expect their rents to stay at affordable levels, again as long as they manage their income efficiently. And they can expect some degree of overall security in terms of belonging to a co-operative society – one for all and all for one. The personal benefits are things like being with like-minded people, acquiring skills, not being hassled by a private landlord, and being valued for one's contribution.

These benefits must be seen to be equally available to everyone. Unfortunately it sometimes happens that the long-term members, or the ones who do most work, or the ones with the loudest voices, or in the worst situation, or the ones whose cousin works for

the builders, get more out of the co-op than the rest.
They'll get the house with the south-facing garden,
the extra shelving in the kitchen, or even a few quid
more on their expense claim. It happens. But, it can
be prevented if every single scrap of co-op activity
is done in the public arena of meetings and is fully
reported in minutes, and if every member knows they
have a right to ask questions. It is also prevented if all
members are committed to the principle of equality

iii) How do they benefit collectively?

The collective economic benefits of the co-operative
are obvious. Rental income is used to pay the mortgage, cover day-to-day repair, the costs of producing
a newsletter, paying for the office phone, and paying
the staff. Surpluses are usually allocated annually
to long-term maintenance or improvement funds, or
specialist childcare so parents with disabled kids can
attend meetings. But if you're very prudent, annual
parties and outings, buying laptops for every house
or a co-op minibus are not impossible achievements.

However, the actual Principle itself reads *"benefiting
members in proportion to their transactions with the
co-operative"*. This is more appropriate in worker's
co-ops where the members may decide to put a proportion of the profits into a trust. Usually the allocation
of trust money is limited to longer term members. But
in a housing co-op, the whole belongs to the whole,
whatever the input. Economic input may also refer to
time and energy. The only time where reward for greater
input (i.e. benefiting in proportion to transactions)
is sometimes used in co-ops is in choosing who gets
the brand new flat, or first refusal on a self-contained
transfer. Members who have put in more time and effort
clock up more points and would have a better chance.

Rewarding participation can cause problems though.
One danger is that members who are highly committed but less able to participate, because of work
or study or childcare, may lose out. And incentives
which kindled someone's desire to contribute may
evaporate once they've been housed. The co-op must
decide these issues for itself, but should never lose
sight of the underlying basis of shared equity.

The commitment to equality is aimed at shared equity,
which will only be achieved through the application
of the first two principles. And whilst shared equity
primarily refers to cash or capital, and secondarily to

the more intangible benefits such as community and group support, it is the objective of the commitment to equality that each member makes when they join a co-operative. Through compromise and democracy a co-op really can achieve an equitable collective life.

Commitment 2 – Unity

Fourth Co-operative Principle of Autonomy and Independence

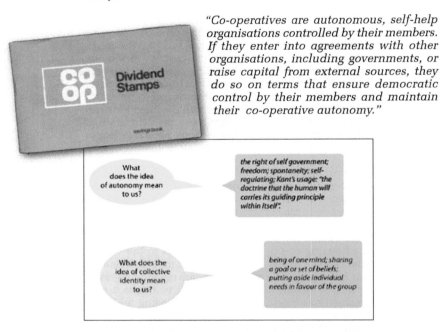

"Co-operatives are autonomous, self-help organisations controlled by their members. If they enter into agreements with other organisations, including governments, or raise capital from external sources, they do so on terms that ensure democratic control by their members and maintain their co-operative autonomy."

What does the idea of autonomy mean to us?

the right of self government; freedom; spontaneity; self-regulating; Kant's usage: "the doctrine that the human will carries its guiding principle within itself".

What does the idea of collective identity mean to us?

being of one mind; sharing a goal or set of beliefs; putting aside individual needs in favour of the group

Holding the centre together in a hostile world

The fourth principle of autonomy and independence is a tricky one. The first sentence is fine, it's the rest of it which is harder to grasp... Firstly, co-ops unquestionably exist in a world not of their own making. However co-operative the co-op manages to be internally, on its own ground, on its own terms, it is still confronted by the fact that the outside world, including the funders and regulators, is governed by a completely different set of principles. The truth is that the outside world is allowing the co-op to exist. It will only continue to do so if the co-op conforms to the standards it sets. Co-ops are curious beasts which are tolerated but need to be kept under control. They symbolise a transgression against the principles upon which the rest of the world is set up. So, how can a co-op fulfil this principle, and remain true to itself?

The co-op's objectives can promote internal cohesion

It is precisely the clear cut distinction between the interests of a co-operative and the interests of the external world which draws the collective membership into a group identity and a unity of purpose. It must never be forgotten that setting up a co-op in an essentially hostile environment took considerable struggle and enormous commitment on the part of the founder members. The founders had to develop a sense of collective identity in order to succeed. It's a case of everyone pulling in the same direction. Housing Co-ops actually are the horse designed by a committee!

Maintaining a sense of group purpose preserves its autonomy

Creating a collective identity is a practical job. Initiating and building something is of course practical but the excitement of the project inspires an energetic determination to succeed. This also stirs a strong sense of independence and autonomy in people because they feel as if they are doing battle. The problems of maintaining a unified sense of purpose and direction, and of continually reasserting the autonomy of a co-op, grow from the inevitable relaxation that comes about when the houses are built. The members are happily benefiting from the plumbing that works, the delicious central heating, and the sense of security in belonging to a co-operative. What gets forgotten is that keeping it all going is still a struggle. The regulators just keep on thinking of new ways to make life difficult. The bills keep coming in. Voids arise and have to be filled. The central heating needs to have regular servicing or one day pressing that button won't have the desired effect.

The threat of change can undermine autonomy

Bringing in new members can also affect the co-op's sense of having one mind geared towards fulfilling its goal. If change is not integrated into co-op life, the internal glue holding the co-op together can come unstuck. Change can threaten continuity, unless older members are willing to move with the times. It can be difficult for the oldies not to feel protective and parental about their baby housing co-op. It's right that they should, but they must avoid overdoing it. If they do, the co-op will not so much be threatened by the new blood, but by the fears of the older generation. Change can be managed by taking the opportunity to re-evaluate the co-op's current state, which can involve all the members. The perceptions of new members can be extraordinarily revealing, and should be welcomed.

Democratic control must be demonstrated

Collective autonomy is achieved through reaching consensus, or at least a convincing majority, and developing a group mind, and group commitment to the idea. The co-op has to be able to say to the outside world that it collectively backs the actions taken on its behalf. This is achieved through voting at meetings, and having clear written records of such voting. This is the mechanism for "ensuring democratic control by their members", and speaks both ways. Primarily, the Society is accountable to its membership, and without meetings and minutes, the membership cannot be in control. Secondarily, if the membership cannot be seen to be in control, the outside world need not take it seriously, and indeed can step in and abolish its autonomy.

Practical example of how to be autonomous

A simple example of this is in dealing with the bank. The bank has issued a cheque book for the use of the Society. But the Society must be represented to the bank by a number of delegated signatories. The bank will not honour cheques unless it has a record that those signatories have been thus delegated. It wants to see the minutes of the meeting which approved the delegation. No minutes, no cash. No cash, no action, no autonomy. No autonomy, no unity, no co-op.

Fifth Co-operative Principle of Education, Training and Information

"Co-operatives provide education and training for their members, elected representatives, managers and employees so they can contribute effectively to the development of the co-operative. They inform the general public – particularly young people and opinion leaders – about the nature and benefits of co-operation."

Understanding your world makes you feel you belong in it

One of the things which can interest people in wanting to join a co-op is their hope that they will find not only a house to live in, but a home, somewhere they belong. Society has become fragmented, as the nuclear family has replaced the extended family, and employment is in the office rather than on the land. Very often people feel they don't really belong anywhere, and apart from the few who are at ease with solitude, the majority want some approximation of a family, a community.

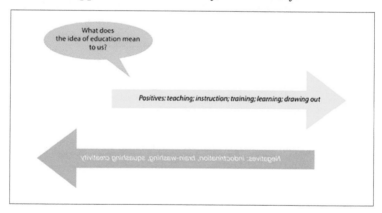

What does the idea of education mean to us?

Positives: teaching; instruction; training; learning; drawing out

Negatives: indoctrination, brain-washing, squashing creativity

Developing friendships in a co-op promotes understanding and belonging

A housing co-op is not under any obligation to provide this, of course. But very often it happens anyway. You keep seeing the same people at meetings, you go for a drink afterwards, you tell each other what you do, what you dream about doing, you become friends. The difference between making friends through a housing co-op and any other way you might make friends is that there is something that is bigger than both of you – the co-op. You find that your friendship is growing while you try to figure out how to write a

Sustainability Policy, or choose which contractor is the best one to renovate the lovely little terraced house you're both going to share.

The threat of divided interest

Education, training and spreading information are absolutely vital activities in a co-op. As a package, they enable members to reach a shared understanding of the co-op's overall objectives and the issues the co-op deals with. Without these three things operating on a regular basis, members can go off in little cliques and become out of touch with each other. There will and should be differences of opinion, but they need to be aired in the group. Otherwise, opinions can become inflexible, and clashes will arise. Co-ops are not a bed of roses where everything is sweetness and light, but neither should they be battlegrounds for dogmatists. Compromise is the essential component but people will only compromise if they feel their views have been heard and appreciated. Communication and meeting skills are the key.

How do we promote understanding?

So, how can the co-op nurture its members, and help them belong to the group and encourage that collective identity so necessary to co-op life? By not taking anything for granted, and making sure that they understand how their co-op works. Do they understand the terms of their fully mutual contractual tenancy; how to pay their rent, and get a repair done; how a new member may come to live in their home; what to do if they don't understand?! And then, do they understand the co-op principles, the origins of their co-op and the co-op movement, and the potential for a fairer, safer future?

Education helps members find their place in the scheme of things

Co-op education is not like school education. School is on the whole about stuffing heads full of facts and formulae, about smoothing out the last kinks of individuality and turning out a malleable workforce. There are facts to absorb in a co-op, but there is a direct application. A co-operative needs people who will take the initiative, and yet work well with each other. People who are not afraid to ask because they are not going to be told they're stupid. Co-operative education is about drawing out people's natural abilities and finding a place for them in the life of the co-op. Not only will the co-op provide a physical home but it can also come to be where they can fit themselves in. And the skills they learn will be useful outside the co-op too; hard skills like bookkeeping, word processing, drawing up maintenance specifications, even office filing, and soft skills like listening, assertiveness, and negotiating.

Co-operative education is about drawing out people's natural abilities and finding a place for them in the life of the co-op

Development and expansion through education

From the sense of belonging which can be nurtured through an enlightened education programme, members can be encouraged to look outside the immediate environment and put the second part of this principle into practise, namely to "inform the general public – particularly to young people and opinion leaders – about the nature and benefits of co-operation". This part of the principle is often put on the back burner as so much energy has to go into the day to day running of the co-op. But, needless to say, if we are to put the sixth and seventh principles into practice, spreading the word to the outside world is the first step. This does not mean going out on a crusade. But running regular New Members meetings and the occasional public meeting, printing leaflets, getting into the local papers, are all ways of spreading the word.

Education will secure the co-op's future

The ongoing provision of education, training and information is essential if the co-op is not only to enable its members to take part, but to ensure the perpetuation of the co-operative idea itself. Without it, we, as member-tenants, and the movement as a whole, will simply not have a secure future.

Commitment 3 – Security

Co-operation brings security

People turn to co-operation because they have realised that the world is a pretty insecure place without it. It's an instinctive realisation, usually not founded in a social, economic, political analysis of the world. This realisation does not necessarily arrive in the new member's head the day they buy their share. At that point they often do not really understand what buying that share actually means. Often, they have joined the co-op because of the low rent, because of the community, the great parties, the sense of freedom. But there are some stunning co-ops around the country which have, for instance, saved the terraces where they have lived all their lives, threatened because of the closure of a coal mine to which the property was tied, or because the council was strapped for cash. These co-ops bring a particular reality to the pursuit of security, because they are set up by people whose existing communities were facing extinction. And they have great parties too!

Following the Co-operative Principles

Whatever the original reasons for setting up the co-op, whatever the particular threat might have been, a co-operative will only become and remain secure if the members follow the co-operative principles. The struggle goes on, and member participation should be acknowledged as a condition of membership.

---

* *More than 1 billion co-operative members*
* *More than 12% of humanity is part of any of the 3 million cooperatives in the world!*
* *The largest 300 co-operatives and mutuals report a total turnover of $2,034.98Bn*
* *Co-operatives contribute to the sustainable economic growth and stable, quality employment, employing 280 million people across the globe, in other words, 10% of the world's employed population.*

Facts from Co-operatives UK

Sixth Co-operative Principle of Co-operation among Co-operatives

"Co-operatives serve their members most effectively and strengthen the co-operative movement by working together through local, regional, national, and international structures."

Collaboration

It's been said that "we need to live the vision, the objectives, the values, and stand up and be counted as co-operators." But does this business about standing up and being counted give the project a political flavour? And isn't co-operativism supposed to be apolitical? Yes, in the sense that the first principle demands that co-ops are open to anyone, whatever their views. But, in the sense of 'political' as involvement in civic life, that is, in taking responsibility for the community and pursuing its best interests, co-operativism is a political activity. How can it be otherwise, when it is set up as an alternative to the status quo?

Co-ops are like flocks of starlings. At a certain moment, a trigger, the individual birds engage together in a sky dance of swirling, coagulating, swooping, curling movement, deciding together where the safest place to sleep is, where they can look out for each as a tribe, because they know they are safer as part of the collective. Co-ops have the same psychology, each one is individual, with its own history and resources, but each knows also that the other co-ops around it follow the same principles and have the same aims. Over time, they pull together and drift apart, according to the currents.

This means that the work of collaboration must be constant through the fervent times and the dormant periods. Collaboration is the equivalent of the air, always present but in different forms, still, humid, blustery, it is the movement. What greater security could we all have than through pooling our resources and knowledge and bringing about a co-operative revolution?

Toad Lane, Rochdale, the first co-op shop

Can we change the world?

The mechanisms are in place, for co-operation among co-operatives, in all of the above categories – surviving and flourishing housing co-ops, local community land trusts (CLTs), both with local and national bodies lobbying on their behalf, Radical Routes, Catalyst Collective, The Co-operative College, Co-operativesUK, and the

International Co-operative Alliance, set up in 1895...
why haven't we changed the world yet? Well, it's either
because THEY are bigger than US, or because we have
not quite realised the potential. It's probably a bit of both.

The potential for change

The potential is staggering. There are 1 billion co-op
members in some 3 million co-ops across the world.
There are many worker co-ops all over the UK, across
agricultural co-ops, and fishing, milk production
and distribution, publishing and printing, furniture
making and upholstery, film making, medical care,
are all fields where co-operators have provided community services and reaped the benefits.

Does the co-op want to change the world?

Robert Owen, the 19th century exponent of the idea,
claimed co-operativism had universal application, and
that society could become co-operative. Co-operativism
is 'a tool to influence positively the local community
and thereby, change society'. But changing the world
is a formidable task! Before we reach for the stars, we
need to reach each other on a small scale. Working
through the previous five principles will give a co-op
the foundation to begin addressing the sixth. Through
compromise, democracy, shared equity, collective
identity and belonging through understanding, the
co-op can start to look at involvement in the co-
operative movement.

Organisation and delegation

The Sixth Principle depends entirely on members'
ability to organise themselves, which is a vital aspect
of participation. This ability first proves itself in the
everyday management of the co-op, but this can be so
demanding that the higher ideals don't get a look in.
There is a very strong case for establishing within each
co-op a group dedicated to the sixth principle. Often we
find that co-ops concentrate their resources on running

ica

COOP
International
Co-operative
Alliance

the maintenance programme, or supervising lettings, etc., which is understandable. But not looking outside to the co-op movement, or the co-operative principles, for opportunities for collaboration will eventually disable the co-op. When this kind of isolation happens, they will carry on for years unable to solve problems, and living in a state of perpetual crisis management. Setting up a specific group will allow the co-op to explore its connections to other co-ops, and develop an organisational strategy for strengthening the movement.

Getting to know other co-ops

The starting point for this is making connections with other co-ops in the area, and pooling whatever resources are available. Two Piers, for instance, had members who wanted to set up a new shortlife. At this time, Two Piers had received a rather large and unusual present from the Housing Corporation, in the shape of £5,000, free, gratis and entirely the co-op's to do use as it wanted. Two Piers set up a Development Loan Fund, so other fledgling co-ops could register as friendly societies. Through this, a couple of dozen new co-ops were founded, and the local network CHIBAH (Co-operative Housing In Brighton And Hove) was formed.

Although this is an unusual story, contacting other local co-ops and pooling resources can bring all the benefits of collaboration. Some would say keep it local or regional, that the national scale is too big. "The larger the entity the smaller the participation by members in proportion to the total membership, and the less they represent the real interests of their members". If this is the case, maybe the reason is that our horizons can only extend so far, and beyond whatever this boundary may be, things just get vague and disconnected. But, if we could take on whatever we think we can manage, we might succeed.

Seventh Co-operative Principle of Concern for Community

"Co-operatives work for the sustainable development of their communities through policies approved by their members."[1]

All seven quotes featured in this article are the Co-operative Principles as stated by the International Co-operative Alliance in 1995

Sustainable development

And here we have it – the caring, sharing co-op. As a child I used to parrot this little catchphrase, not under-standing how the high street shop with the blue and white logo did care and share. Perhaps if The Co-op had had posters up with pictures of people helping each other and getting things done together, I might have got the message.

The seventh principle was added to the other six in 1995. Perhaps it just didn't seem that obvious. But now the world is in such dire straits we have to consciously dedicate some time to looking after the interests of our communities.

So, what's going on in this area?

Community bicycle scheme? Electric car co-op? Wholefood shops? Alternative health and community care? Permaculture initiatives? Childcare? What do the members need and can fellow co-ops provide for them?

How can policies be developed?

Before setting out to take on the whole of Agenda 21, the co-op must consider what resources it has available, both in terms of time and money. More importantly though, is the need to think in the long term, tricky at any time, but more so for a co-op which has so far just been fixing the roof and chasing the rent arrears. How long is the 'long term' anyway?

Co-operative housing is about stewarding land and property in perpetuity, and perpetui-ty doesn't have a sell-by date. When we think about 'stewarding' though, it evokes a sense of acquiring deep knowledge of the ecology of the thing we are, essentially, protect-ing. This is not unlike bringing up children – figuring out how they tick and helping them flourish. So part of stewarding is to ensure that the stewards really know the terrain, and develop responses to opportunities or threats. Another part is understanding how external factors also evolve.

UN Sustainable Development statement from the United Nations Conference on Environment & Development, Rio de Janeiro, Brazil, 3 to 14 June 1992

Agenda 21 - Chapter 1 PREAMBLE
1.1. Humanity stands at a defining moment in history. We are confronted with a perpetuation of disparities between and within nations, a worsening of poverty, hunger, ill health and illiteracy, and the continuing deterioration of the ecosystems on which we depend for our well-being. However, integration of environment and development concerns and greater attention to them will lead to the fulfilment of basic needs, improved living standards for all, better protected and managed ecosystems and a safer, more prosperous future. No nation can achieve this on its own; but together we can - in a global partnership for sustainable development.

Developing policy needs much careful consideration, to avoid committing the co-op to an impossible task. Start off small, and succeed. Invite a speaker to talk on an issue which grabs the members' interest. Visit a scheme or local environmental group, exchange information and ideas. Remember that members engaged in this activity are contributing their time and energy, and ensure their participation is recognised.

6. Concern for Community: Sustainability
The Development Group shall:
6.1 Promote, support and facilitate the growth of This Co-op's members in their understanding of housing management by organising:
a) training on how to participate in co-operative management
b) debate on what co-operation and Co-operativism mean in day to day life and in the wider world: "Co-operatives are jointly owned and democratically controlled enterprises rooted in the values of self-help, self-responsibility, equality, equity, democracy, and solidarity. People, not profit, are at the centre of a co-operative's economic activity."
c) learning about succession planning and focusing on training members to replace existing post holders
6.2 Encourage all other management groups to engage in sustainability issues
6.3 Facilitate training in grant applications and/or access to knowledge about sustainability, including attending conferences

Two Piers Development Group Terms of Reference (under review at time of publication)

Summary

To make participation as a co-operative member real and meaningful, it has to embody:

- A co-operative society which is meaningful to me in geographical, cultural or ethnic terms; something with which I can identify – 'that's my Society, it has my values, we use it and we have a disproportionate influence on my neighbourhood.'

- My ability to participate and influence.

- My opportunity to benefit from such membership in cash terms and/or in terms of the society and environment in which I wish my family and I to live.

Home: Helen's lovely home in Two Piers Housing Co-op

Maintenance: 1980s single glazing being replaced

participation: late ME. [-(O)Fr. participation - late L. participatio, capere - to take, pars - part, f. as prec.: see -ION.] 1. The action or fact of partaking, having or forming part of; †the partaking of the substance, quality, or nature of. 2. The fact or condition of sharing in common (with others, or each other): partnership, fellowship; profit-sharing; late ME. b. A taking part (with others) in some action or matter 1667.

"Sharing in whatever surplus profits are realised by the more efficient labour which participation calls forth." (1881) Shorter O.E.D.

Participation: The definition of participation shows it's give and take

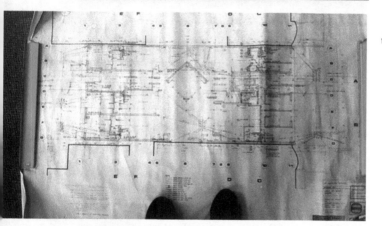

Plans: It all starts with a plan!

Meeting: Behind the scenes where the work gets done

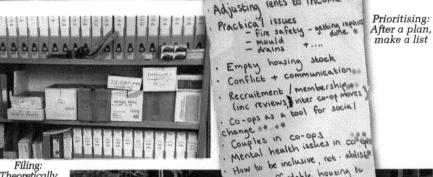

Filing: Theoretically we know where stuff is!

Adjusting rents to income

Practical issues
 - fire safety - getting repairs done
 - mould +....
 - drains

- Empty housing stock
- Conflict + communication
- Recruitment / membership (inc reviews, inter co-op moves)
- Co-ops as a tool for social change
- Couples in co-ops
- Mental health issues in co-op
- How to be inclusive, not ablist
- Offering affordable housing to people who really need it.

Prioritising: After a plan, make a list

Relaxing: That lovely moment when the list is sorted and we can talk about something else!

Helen Russell

joined Two Piers Housing Co-operative in 1983, and was Chair during the development of the co-op's new build. She helped set up new co-ops, was acting Chair of the old NFHC 1989-1990, and collaborated with other co-ops in founding CCH 1991-1993. Helen has undertaken policy review, training of members, representing Two Piers at the local housing co-op network, CHIBAH, and at the national network CCH. Helen is a founder member of the Brighton & Hove Community Land Trust. She is a piano teacher and composer, a mum, grows tomatoes and watches a lot of Korean TV dramas. [helen@chibah.org]. This article was originally written by Helen in 1992 and revised in 2020 and 2022.

Helen running a promo stall

Number 25: Radical Hospitality

MIM SKINNER

What if you opened your home to anyone who needed it? Along with her housemates, author Mim Skinner did just that...

It may seem odd to pick up a book about urban communities and come to a chapter amongst these pages of thriving collectivist hubs which details a community which came and went relatively quickly.

Like many others who've trodden similar paths though, I don't tell the story of our community in terms of its failure. Those years that our community house ran it was both catalyst and chaos, and the most incredibly life-affirming home to spend my twenties in. We started without a ten year plan or aspirations toward one and named ourselves simply after our house number – Number 25.

In its brevity the experience does, perhaps, speak to a recurring theme in communities similar to ours. That urban residential projects intermingled with activism and cheap shared housing often flare up, burn brightly and die away. That many communities like our own which are very outward-focussed, open-doored and tightly-packed into family sized homes repurposed with bunk beds and curtain-dividers launch their residents onto a longer road rather than providing sustainable housing options for life. It was a place of large parties, big ideas and cyclical burn-outs.

Our founding members met at an event called 'Dreams' where Christians of a wide range of backgrounds, traditions and beliefs met together to share their dreams for the City and wider County of Durham. From grassroots political movements to green revolution, Church unity to improved town-gown collaboration.

A student I didn't really know shared his discomfort with the idea that the City had a number of homeless people whilst others had spare rooms. What would it look like, he asked, if we made our spare rooms available to those that needed them? I spoke similarly about what 'radical hospitality' might look like, inviting those on the outskirts of communities into the centre. In the room that evening was a local landlord, and a handful

of youth workers, political activists, and recent graduates filling time working in coffee shops. We gravitated together afterwards to speak more.

That group became our founding members, and the landlord's house, our base, a five bedroom end-of-terrace house near the City centre. We spent the following months drinking

Homemade props for our community's voter registration campaign

enormous quantities of tea in those ubiquitous Sports Direct mugs that peppered every student house. We sketched out our life together in marker pens and A3 flip chart pads, using different coloured pens for our internal practices and external priorities.

We trained as hosts with the charity Nightstop Depaul so we could receive referrals for emergency accommodation and asked others to join us. Those who felt they needed their own room were given one, and the rest of us shared. We each paid £67 a week in rent and split bills equally so it was an extremely cheap way to live.

In advance of moving in we designed in a rhythm of mealtimes, prayer and meditation, hospitality and activism. Each evening, apart from our one 'house-only' night a week, there was a meal to which anybody could be invited. Each weekday morning began with fifteen minutes of prayer taken from Shane Claibourne's 'Common Prayer, a liturgy for ordinary radicals'. Within the category of 'Christian' we occupied the broadest spectrum, from deconstructing liberals who spoke of God in she/they pronouns to those who went to churches run by male-only eldership. In between were mystic Catholics, evangelicals, recovering evangelicals and admirers of the Northern Saints. We met at the meal-table where rituals of liturgy, lit candles and broken bread provided a meeting point in the centre of our disparities. We hosted regular creative-sharing nights where people came and whistled theme songs, read from text books and improvised skits. I lived on a top bunk, dressed from a shared wardrobe and had only a handful of possessions that were mine alone.

It began with a slow start. A few of us ran a soup kitchen in the town centre so had a fairly good idea of who it was safe to invite to

Music in the garden

stay with us. We hoped to be able to provide a place of safety but draw our line of risk slightly left of someone making off with our telly.

I proudly offered a bed to Albert, a man in his eighties who slept in a doorway in town, and he politely declined. Our ambitious and radical plans which had been writ large in marker pen suddenly felt a little naive. Did people even need our spare room? Would they want to live with us?

Our first guest was the most wonderful young woman from the US who needed a few weeks' accommodation. She was from a mennonite tradition so wore a long skirt and a headscarf. She found us at our worst. The moving process coupled with illness and sudden overwhelming proximity meant that having promised community, we had little energy for her. After talking about how we would provide welcome to those that needed it, we found that she was a source of kindness and stability for us. She cooked

Community gardening (variably successful)

us food and washed towels as we learnt to settle in and live alongside each other. She provided calm words and quiet prayer in the rush of newness.

It was often full in those first months – we had plenty of aimless graduates, visiting friends and people in tenancy gaps, those just needing to retreat from the spin of life, but unsurprisingly our keenest hopes did not immediately materialise because we had a room to house them.

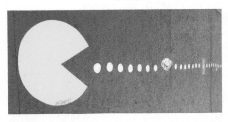

Wheat-paste grafitti on a nearby building site. A comment on the University's fossil fuel investments

Our emergency referrals eventually came for one, two and three nights, but only until accommodation was provided. I had an ill-advised fling with one of our guests, a friend who had recently graduated and was staying whilst plotting his next move. I remember thinking, "This is all perfectly nice, but I don't actually think a live-in love-interest sponsored by my housemates was what any of us had in mind when we drew our plans together." I felt a little embarrassed when people who'd heard us speak at the Dreams event, asked how it was all going.

It did though, after a while, gain momentum. Our dinner table required its expanding panel and it became a reflex to cook for ten or twelve each night, great pots of stew that could be bulked out easily for the unexpected diners we knew would come.

Our first longer term guest, a 19 year old who had been street homeless, came to us for five months, and has remained a friend for many years since. Whilst it sounds like the disingenuous words of a minor celebrity visiting an orphanage in 'Africa' (country not specified), he really did teach us more than we taught him. We learnt what it was like to live alongside one another. He brought new ideas and skills, and we offered some stability. He taught me to skin and cook a squirrel, and we taught him about cleaning rotas and came to housing appointments with him.

He gave our activism some focus; he joined us to campaign about NHS privatisation, registered himself to vote and introduced ground coffee to the woodwork centre where he was a trainee. He reared a bald and shut-eyed magpie chick in his bedroom, that someone aptly described as a 'scrotum with a beak', and built a pallet campsite in the woods behind our house. He moved into his own house after 5 months but left us with the habits of hospitality. We continued to house people but in our grown confidence we became more comfortable with pauses and empty periods, more comfortable with the mix of emergency guests and visiting friends.

Number 25 was both an exciting place to be and an exhausting one, particularly for the introverts amongst us. One of our residents became very unwell with ME shortly before moving in and found the pacing her condition required to maintain stores of energy was made difficult by the unpredictable cycles of activity over which none of us had much control. An impromptu gathering of people in the communal space could leave you confined to your room if you needed to pause and rest. If you'd planned to sit on the sofa and not have to expend any social energy then this was particularly annoying.

The other side of that coin was that frenetic energy could also be incredibly productive. I'm amazed at the number of ideas, projects and campaigns that grew out of conversations had in that kitchen.

Often the people attracted to the house meals, who orbited the rhythms were activist types in search of a home for their hope. We were able to be a gathering point for some of that energy locally.

On any given day we lurched between stupid and profound, earnest and absurd. I remember my sister once visited and though it was several months since her birthday we threw her a Hawaiian Star Wars party where a sleeping-bag Jabba the Hut shared questionable punch with several lei-wearing Leias. We were drunk on our sense of solidarity, free to be both stupid and daring.

Food waste collected for our community meals

Connections were made which turned into friendships and projects, that challenged assumptions and changed perspectives. A roll of black sacks lived by the door, ready for our regular midnight trips to the supermarket bins where we'd intercept food from landfill to cook up into large community dinners. First in the house and then in borrowed community spaces. We painted protest banners on the dining table, held our own version of TED Talks in local cafes sharing ideas on

social justice and community change. We plastered
construction boards near the house with wheat-pasted
climate change art and earned a visit from the community police after we wrote in rainbow chalk across
the house's external wall 'to love another person is to
see the face of God'.

Those who chose to join the community or visit us
often had in common the audacity of believing that
a better, different world was possible, and the even
greater audacity of believing we could help to bring
that world about.

A gathering for someone's baptism.

More than half the ideas that passed through the front
door failed. We ran events with a handful of attendees
and gigs where we played to ourselves. There were
projects that were piloted and then died a death. But
some didn't. Our bin-diving community meals turned
into a food intercepting organisation, REfUSE CIC,
founded on our top bunk with a bitten-ended biro. It
now runs a large warehouse, cafe and catering company
that collects 13 tonnes of food each month, redirects it
to local communities and trains people into employment who have barriers to inclusion.

Discussions about ethical media spawned a grass-roots
tabloid, training citizen journalists to tell their own
stories. It ran for while, anyway.

Some round the table moved from local activism to
party politics. My partner Sam founded a refugee choir
with Syrian young people that went on to tour the UK,
performed in Parliament and released an album. We
planted an allotment with young people on a nearby
estate and registered others to vote for the first time,
wearing fancy-dress in the marketplace. The collec-

tive 'Yes We Can' spirit expanded our perception of what was possible.

It's not hard to pick up from reading this how much affection I have for that time in my life. It is, of course, finely filtered through the rose tint of nostalgia. I may not have waxed so consistently lyrical during my time there. It could be cliquey, difficult for quieter voices to be heard amid the clamour and hard to boundary your energy. I felt like I was never not washing sheets, never not washing up.

Some of the housemates throw a birthday party

But to live according to the maxim 'fuck it, why not?' And to do so in supportive company, can be as wonderful as it is unsustainable, as fun as it is draining. To have my world shaped by so many people from so many different corners of human experiences was such a gift. The community provided a place of safety to live in constant conversation with my Christian faith, along with all of its doubts and nuances, at a time I was beginning to deconstruct the hierarchies and structures of my Church upbringing.

The truth is though, that despite all the fondness I feel for that time, at some point it didn't work for us anymore and we chose to move on. I found myself getting weary. Six years later, our ideas had turned into companies we were then responsible for running, funding and safeguarding, which demanded a consistency that the fervour of starting them off had not. I wanted to have a cup of tea in peace without having to have a conversation about the Universal Basic Income or veganism with whoever happened to be in the kitchen. I wanted to plan my afternoon without an unexpected knocker wanting a sandwich or a shower.

The dining room transformed into an audience for a creative sharing night

Alongside the permanence of our growing projects, as I approached my thirties, an unexpected urge to start

The housemates throwing a birthday party.

a pension and get on the property ladder came over me. When we got married, my husband Sam and I swapped that life in for a quieter, more predictable one with our cat and loft conversion. I walked round bathroom showrooms as though they were art galleries and bought Farrow&Ball tester pots in eight shades of green.

It's the communal cooking that has been the hardest habit to break. In those early days of living as a two, meals would fill our two plates and then Tupperware boxes and cling-filmed bowls with food destined for phantom unexpected guests, as if I was still exercising an amputated limb.

That community that birthed us into the adults we are now will leave its imprint forever. Our former housemates are now our daughter's Godparents. We meet for dinner every week and still campaign together and pray together. The food waste project which started with us perfecting the two person 'wheelie barrow' move to hoist one another into supermarket bins is now run by 13 staff and over 200 volunteers.

After a few years resting we're designing again on napkin backs how we can live in more open and conjoined ways. This time, more balanced, longer-planned and with families in tow.

Mim Skinner
is an author and social enterprise founder living in County Durham. Her debut book *Jailbirds* was one of *Stylist*'s books of the year for 2020 and won her a place on *Elle Magazine*'s list of 50 Game Changers. She's written for The Sunday Times, *The Guardian*, *The i* and *The Huffington Post*. Her most recent book *Living Together* is about touring UK intentional communities and her own journey to living communally again with her husband and daughter.

Urban Rented Communities

NOAH WALTON

Community doesn't have to be for life. What if you could just try it out for a bit? Urban communard Noah spills the beans on his four-part framework and reveals secrets for thriving.

A relearning

In Western societies, it is uncommon to grow up in communal living arrangements. The norm is now to live in small nuclear families or alone. As society has industrialised, we have lost some of the skills required for successful communal living. We need to take the time to re-learn these skills.

Over the past decade, I have been exploring this through the experience of creating and living in a number of intentional communities in London. This chapter explores the secrets learned from the simple and repeatable models of urban rented communal living. I'll first discuss how 'common-sense' principles from normative romantic relationships can be applied to communities, then examine why communities often fail. Finally, we will look at four keys to creating a healthy intentional community drawn from Diana Leafe Christian's work: a clear vision; nurturing the "glue" that holds people together; creating agreements to avoid structural conflicts; and learning skills to handle interpersonal conflicts.

Why live in a community?

If you are this far into a book about community living, you may already know full-well why community living might be desirable. Practical reasons that I have experienced for living in community include:

- Communities can help to sustain social change, and model the world we want to see. (It's not a coincidence that Gandhi spent most of his time living in ashrams.)

- We can have more emotional support in our lives. There are opportunities for friendships, reduced loneliness, a sense of belonging. Living in a community can have a profound impact on our well-being, as our presence together can help to regulate each other's emotions.

- We can have both a healthy material abundance and lower environmental impact when we share with each other.

- It is more fun. There are more social opportunities, connections and conversations. It feels like we enrich each other's lives.

- It saves time. We share household tasks like cleaning and cooking. We each clean once a week, and have a rotation of tasks. The bathrooms get cleaned every week, but we each have to clean them once every six weeks! Similarly, we can all eat a home-cooked dinner most nights, but only have to cook dinner once a week.

- It is cheaper. Utility bills are a fraction of the cost. We buy food in bulk. Because we share spaces we can afford to have communal spaces that we couldn't necessarily afford by ourselves: a nice kitchen, living room and small garden. In the last community I lived in we were lucky enough to have a second living room solely dedicated as a meditation yoga space. It is easier to put up guests, as there is often a spare room available.

The relationship metaphor

In a long-term relationship, we share many aspects of our lives, including a living space, countless meals, social connections, financial ties, dreams, childcare, good and bad habits, and physical intimacy. All of these aspects, with the typical exception of physical intimacy, are commonly shared by people living in intentional communities.

We learn the prevailing wisdom involved in successful romantic relationships from a young age. We absorb ideas from our parents, TV shows, articles, social media, and endless conversations with our peers. Despite such extensive study, 50% of supposedly-permanent marriages still fail. Given the lower level of effort put into learning about intentional communities, it is not surprising that their failure rate is even higher at 80% to 90%.

A fixation on permanence

People grow, change, have varying needs, and this may lead to them falling in and out of love with people and communities, just like they do in relationships. Is it realistic to expect that your first romantic partner will be the person you want to be with for the rest of your life? Similarly, is it reasonable to believe that your first serious intentional community will be the one you want to live in forever?

In our society, there is often a notion that relationships must last forever in order to be considered successful. However, this is a fixed view that may not always align with individuals' evolving needs and desires. Why do we have a tendency to look back at past relationships (and communities) as failures while tending to look back more fondly at old friendships? Can we set our expectations realistically at the outset, to enable any future loosening of the connection to happen in an emotionally safer way?

Damanhur, a spiritual ecovillage located in Italy, operates under a different philosophy. Its residents are committed to holistic living, spiritual development, and sustainability, and they have a unique approach to relationships and marriage. In Damanhur, couples can choose between either a two-year or five-year marriage, rather than committing to a lifetime union.

What if we applied this same concept to communities? Instead of rapidly committing years of effort and life savings to a forever community, how can we experiment safely? How can we test the waters of living with others before making a long-term commitment? Are we even sure that a permanent community is the right goal to be aiming for? Could a 2-year or a 5-year community actually serve our lives better?

Fixed-term communities provide a win-win in many ways: On the one hand they provide a solid foundation from which a longer term community can healthily grow. On the other hand, they allow a community to change or dissolve peacefully and safely at an appropriate juncture if that is the best way forward.

In one of the communities I lived in, five friends and I embarked on a journey to establish a particular intentional community in South London in 2017. We declared the venture a 'one-year experiment' and committed to living together for at least a year to explore the depth of their community connection that we could create.

To our great joy, our one year experiment lasted for three years and ended on a positive note, with strong friendships and a desire from some to potentially live together again in the future. One of the keys to our successful ending was carefully managing healthy commitment expectations from the start.

The relationship escalator

If someone was to meet a new romantic partner and immediately decided to combine all their resources and commit to purchasing and residing together for decades into the future without first living together, many people would consider it hasty and unwise.

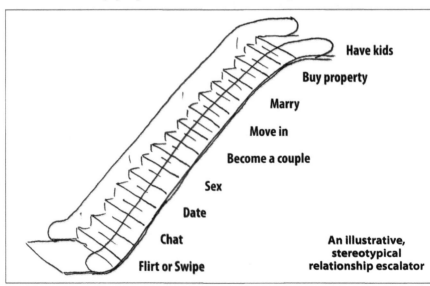

Have kids

Buy property

Marry

Move in

Become a couple

Sex

Date

Chat

Flirt or Swipe

An illustrative, stereotypical relationship escalator

The same line of reasoning could apply to intentional communities who buy property together before they deeply know each other.

In polyamorous circles, there is a useful framework called "the relationship escalator" used to surface and challenge our assumptions about relationship progression. What if two people choose to get married without the expectation of eventually living together? What if two people choose to be a couple but never have sex? There are many beautiful ways to be in the world. What wise/heartfelt way do you want to create for your community?

The Relationship Escalator – used to surface and question assumptions about conventional relationship trajectories – can also be a useful metaphor to unpack intentional community journeys.

Some intentional communities, including ones I have been involved in creating, have consciously chosen to create their own 'community relationship escalator', with stages such as having coffee, eating together, attending workshops and going on holiday, before living together on a temporary then permanent basis. After each stage we have a choice: we are not committed to continuing together, we choose to do so in freedom.

Basic relationship advice can often be applied to communities: Have you considered modelling your community engagement process on your version of a stereotypical romantic courtship? Have you thought about going on holiday together before committing to move in? Occasionally you have to move from the heart, but often a staged process is sound advice.

Failing safely

When communities fail, due to interpersonal conflicts, it can result not only in a loss of relationships and personal hurt, but also risks the material resources and emotional effort invested by members to create the community. The failure of an idealistic community in a bruising and damaging manner can exact a heavy emotional toll and a tragic loss of faith in our idealism to make a positive change in the world.

I have personallyseen too many people who were deeply inspired and excited at the early stages, then hopeless and despondent about how the future looks when it doesn't work out. Creating an intentional community is a complex process, involving multiple individuals, and is much more complex than a binary relationship. It's essential to have a safe and minimally damaging exit route for community members in the early years. Renting communities have lower start-up and exit 'costs' and can offer an emotionally safer route into an intentional community than purchasing a property straight away.

Learn from those that last

There are very few examples of long term communities in our society. If we want to learn processes for how to create sustainable long term communities we need to learn from them. My observation of long term communities that have lasted for generations is that they're quite careful to not let people become full life-long community members immediately. Often, they have a staged, fair process of gradually extended commitments (starting as a two week guest, then becoming a short-term resident, etc.). The whole process usually takes a number of years (a similar length of time to many people's life-partner courtships). From Buddhist monasteries through to successful ecovillages, it seems that similarly long joining processes are used across a wide range of intentional communities that survive the decades.

The most instructive book I have read on community living is *Creating a Life Together – Practical Tools to Grow Ecovillages and Intentional Communities* by Diana Leafe Christian. Learning from the experience of dozens of North American intentional communities over recent decades, she provides valuable practical advice and experience on how to establish a thriving intentional community. The four keys described in the following section are drawn mainly from this book.

Four keys

The high failure rate of intentional communities, with a staggering 80% ending within the first few years, is primarily due to interpersonal issues rather than practical reasons.

It's vital to understand why communities fail, as this gives us the best chance of not failing. It is tempting in our materialistic society to focus on solving "hardware" problems such as property, finances, and environmental sustainability. However, most established communities fail due to interpersonal "software" issues and whether individual members have done the inner work required to live harmoniously in a community.

My experience is that there are four keys to success – drawn largely from Diana Leafe Christian's book – that should be covered as a starting point for intentional communities. They will be explored in this chapter from the perspective of a rented urban intentional community:

1 Strike a clear vision;

2 Work out and deliberately nurture the "glue" that holds you together;

3 Create an agreement for how you're going to live together to avoid Structural Conflicts;

4 Turn towards and learn skills to enable you to grow as a result of Interpersonal Conflicts.

To what extent could these keys also be applicable to other communities and relationships in your life?

1. Strike a clear vision

The foundation of many successful intentional communities is a clear and unwavering vision. This vision should be deeply personal, with a fire of inspiration that keeps burning and motivates you to move forward.

The advice is to "sound a clear note" by being upfront and transparent about priorities and goals, even if it may deter some people. A clear vision will attract like-minded individuals who resonate with it and provide a foundation for a longer journey together. On the other hand, a lack of clarity can result in conflicts and limit the long term potential of the community.

Is your vision one that will be sustainable for decades into the future, or is it time bound? The most successful, lasting intentional communities tend to have visions based on deep shared values, even spiritual beliefs.

What are your reasons for living in a community? Whatever your reasons are can you also build into this personal growth?

Imagine yourself at seventy. Do you want to be someone who is closed minded towards other people or someone who still openly engages with the world? One of the secrets to not getting emotionally stuck in life is community. There is a metaphor for community members being like stones that rub together: rubbing away each other's sharp edges to become smooth over months and years.

I have personally found huge emotional support (and surprisingly even work/livelihood support) from the communities that I have been a part of, and benefited so much from being closely interconnected with other lives on a daily basis. In community life, it is easy to assign costs to the slight loss of time and freedom that we can easily measure: but what is the value of the intangible that a community can offer? The support to stop you falling into depression after a bereavement or a breakup? The people who might be there for you like an extended family?

Taking the time to create a clear and inspiring vision is an essential step in establishing a healthy and thriving community. The clearer and deeper the vision you have, the longer the journey that you can go on together. Similarly, if your vision is unclear in any way, this will often be exactly where unresolvable structural conflict may emerge after a time, and be the limit of how far you can journey together. Creating a vision can be both beautiful and inspiring and – for a group – it's well worth taking a day or a weekend on this process.

Practical alignment

It is easy to fall in love with the idea of community, after a great short-term retreat, event or festival, and have rose-tinted hopes about what it's going to be like. However, is it realistic to imagine that a long-term relationship is going to have a similar energy to a holiday romance?

One question I have heard asked when considering long-term relationships is "how compatible are you on a mundane Wednesday morning?". The same question could be applied to a community.

When determining compatibility as a group seeking to form an intentional community, we often use spectrum exercises. This involves asking individuals to stand somewhere along a 'spectrum' running from one end of the room or the other based on their stance on issues such as:

- Cleanliness preferences (e.g. very relaxed at one end of the room, to meticulous at the other)

- Alcohol consumption

- Attitude towards drug use

- Guests (frequent couchsurfers or a quiet haven)

- Views and preferences on freedom of sexual expression among community members

- Commitment to shared practices (meditation, gardening, communal activities)

- Willingness to share resources (food, for example)

The objective is not to determine the correct answer, but to observe where people stand. For example, it may be acceptable for one person to drink frequently and another to abstain as long as they are both comfortable living together. Or, it may be that these two individuals would be better suited to separate communities (perhaps separate households within a larger network) that better align to each of their preferences or needs.

I developed a rudimentary app where people could assess and rate their own attributes based on two factors for each spectrum: (1) their position, and (2) the importance they placed on others being aligned with them. This generated a playful "% destiny" score for each community member pairing, similar to some dating apps. The outcomes saved a huge amount of time, breaking the ice and initiating discussions around likely areas of compatibility and tension. Groups that I have seen emerge from this kind of process moved forwards with open eyes and grounded expectations.

Inclusivity

In the past, my idealistic nature led me to believe that intentional communities would naturally strive for two goals: to be as inclusive as possible and to provide maximum service to society. I have gradually come to be aware of individuals and their communities' limitations in terms of their capacity. I now reflect more about what resources we have and how to wisely make use of them in a way that balances our own happiness and wellbeing with being of service to the broader community.

I see the various communities in our society as being on a spectrum from inclusive (such as a neighbourhood gardening group) to exclusive (such as most romantic relationships). In the middle we have groups that have certain criteria. A choir could be towards the exclusive end of the spectrum if people have to be able to pass an audition; or inclusive if it is open regardless of ability. An educational institution could be exclusive if it costs a lot and selects students based on who might make a great doctor one day; or inclusive if it is a state-run community school. Some people choose to run their friendship-groups in quite an exclusive manner, while others are more open and happy to go with the flow of who is around them. Where is the most appropriate place for a particular intentional community along this spectrum? Can we go further together to support the world if we create a selective community of highly-aligned, emotionally-attuned people that has minimal internal conflict? Or do most kinds of selection basis simply create a more segregated society?

For a long-term relationship to work well, it is important that the people in the relationship are willing to do sufficient self-reflection to have a healthy and self-aware approach towards each other. While we may wish for everyone to have a romantic relationship if they want one, that doesn't mean that everyone is ready for a relationship or that someone is the right person for us (even if they really want it). What would it mean if we applied this principle to intentional communities?

Diana Leafe Christian's quote "high wounded-ness requires high willing-ness" is apt when it comes to considering people who have interpersonal needs that may impact a community. Given the high rate of failure of intentional communities because of interpersonal breakdown, she advises being mindful of the resources of your community. One wounded person who isn't willing to do their work can be toxic to a community. It is therefore crucial to carefully consider the psychological disposition of those you join together with. This may be subtle and not immediately apparent, which is why (in both relationship and in community) many people choose to live together for a while before making a permanent commitment.

If one member's behaviour requires excessive support or management from other members, it can dangerously drain energy and enthusiasm from the community as a whole. For example, participation in communal activities may become unattractive if one dominant/manipulative member is always present. It's not uncommon for members to realise they cannot handle living with their neighbours only after they have settled in. The stress and anxiety that arises from this realisation can be overwhelming, frequently leading to healthier and more resourced members leaving first, creating a negative feedback loop and making the community fabric less healthy over time.

Many intentional communities have decided to be quite exclusive in who they select, requiring a high-degree of vision alignment, emotional maturity, and having a staged 'dating' process to full membership that is phased over several years. Some intentional communities have aimed to be part of an inclusive community on the neighbourhood scale but decided to allow for more exclusive selection at the household scale. Other intentional communities have decided to be deliberately inclusive, such as the l'Arche communities, where people with and without learning disabilities share lives together.

If we choose to be inclusive or exclusive in some way as a community, it is important to do so extremely consciously. Are the criteria or the processes we are using at risk of unhelpfully retrenching the damaging faultlines and discrimination along the lines of wealth, age, class, race, gender and ability that we have in our society?

2. Work out and deliberately nurture the "glue" that holds you together

With the overarching vision for your community in place, it's crucial to determine the "glue" that holds a community together on a weekly basis. This could be shared activities that people participate in, such as eating together, singing, meditating, gardening, or child-raising. Consider what meaningful contact your community is actually sharing on a day-to-day basis. If you are simply coexisting without any real connection, the community may not feel cohesive.

Many groups in our society call themselves communities nowadays. A brand may even describe itself as having a 'community' of customers who use their products.

Consider a 'community' in a co-working space, for example. Are they eating lunch or sharing in some kind of collective activity regularly? Many of these spaces struggle to foster a real sense of community because people are not actually engaged in shared activities to 'glue' them together. To the degree that 'community' transactions are primarily mediated by money rather than an intention towards a shared common vision and values, the less authentic they will tend to feel.

My experience has been that an optional dinner together each evening for those who are around, combined with a few communal activities (sharing how we are feeling with each other, meditating together, playing music, singing together, running workshops or practising yoga) can work beautifully. Shared projects, such as offering a workshop to the wider community or hosting a party can be excellent ways to bond with each other. Children and gardening can also act as excellent 'glue' to bring a community together, as can social change activism (which can initially be as simple as some local guerrilla gardening).

Humans are cyclical creatures

We see cycles everywhere in society, affecting everybody. Hours, days, weeks, months and years are all cycles. Some cycles are inspired by nature (such as years), while others are social constructs (such as school terms). Our lives are built on cyclical periods of activity and rest: summers for doing, winters for reflection, springs for emerging and autumns for harvesting. Our weeks, too, are formed of days for work and rest. Once you start looking, it can seem that most things we do in our society seem to have a cycle: Everything needs to have a time to "breathe in" and a time to "breathe out". Women, connected with their menstrual cycle, may recognise this more easily than men. If we can support the creation of appropriate cycles, we may find more ease navigating community life.

When agreeing to activities in intentional communities that I have lived in, we used to naively agree to indefinite commitments such as "let's meditate together for half-an-hour every Wednesday morning at 7am". This type of simplistic commitment, stretching indefinitely into the future, quickly started to feel oppressive and claustrophobic. There'd usually be someone in the group who would then feel the need to assert their agency against our agreed commitment in order to not feel trapped.

Once we realised that intentional communities, too, work in cycles, we started to programme activities more wisely: "Let's commit to meditating together for half-an-hour every Wednesday for six weeks, then take two weeks off and evaluate where we want to go from there." Coining activities as a time-bound experiment with the opportunity to be dropped or evolved at the end of a cycle has been incredibly helpful. It has meant that our collective programming more easily aligns with the wise consent/consensus decision-making adage of "good enough for now, safe enough to try", helping to significantly speed up decisions and improve how we feel about them. Liberated from the pressure of immediately creating the perfect structure, we can cyclically iterate our way towards a harmonious supportive community culture.

Holidays, too, are cycles. I have frequently found it useful to take a break from community for a few weeks each year, then feel revitalised when the community is reunited. Often it seems, the trick to relationships/friendships/communities is not so much a binary choice of whether we want them or not in our lives, but what frequency and cyclical pattern is going to fit best. A gardening day every fortnight may become tedious, but a gardening day every quarter may be a sustainable frequency that lasts well into the future. Consider pausing all communal activities for a month each year, so that you can miss it and remember what community offers to your lives.

Sharing food

Eating together is one of the most effective ways to build community. One vitally important rule of thumb is that communities that share more than four meals per week tend to feel more connected. Indeed in ones that don't eat together often enough it can often feel like people are passing each other by like "ships in the night".

We share all our food in the house where I live – something I never thought would work when it was first suggested ten years ago, but has proven itself time and time again in the communities I have lived in to be genuinely brilliant, despite the fact that our lives are healthily independent in many ways.

The advantages are huge – if we each cook once per week, then there is a beautiful meal ready for us at 7pm most nights. There's no necessity that we are always in. There is a beauty with a community of half-a-dozen people in that we have a wonderful, slightly varying group each evening. We simply mark on the blackboard which nights we will be in for dinner.

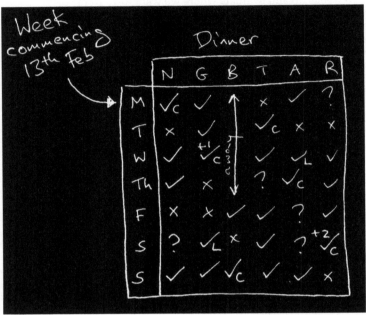

This week's dinner rota copied from our blackboard. We mark when we are cooking ("C"), whether we have any guests ("+1"), or coming back home late wanting leftovers ("L").

For purchases, we use the Splitwise app (free). We are all allowed to purchase whatever food we want for the house, and simply upload the receipts of what we've purchased so that it's tracked and reconciled. If you want to buy orange juice, buy two so that others can have some too and you don't feel the slightest urge to jealously guard it. There is a joy to opening a fridge and knowing you can eat anything.

We have a simple technical rule of "all food is shared unless it is in a bag". If you have made yourself a packed lunch for the next day, or have some ingredients you particularly want to cook with tomorrow night, just make sure to pop it in a bag. For clutter, we developed a lost property basket (affectionately renamed the Tidy Your S#*! box), and pre-permitted anyone to clear things that have been left out off the surfaces.

For cleaning, we aim to leave the kitchen as we find it (unless it is a rare special occasion). For us this means not leaving any dirty dishes next to the sink. We have found that if all six of us each leave a couple of items there, then we quickly have a "tragedy of the commons" style issue, where responsibility for who's cleaning it up isn't quite clear, and resentments can build.

3. Create an agreement for how you're going to live together to avoid Structural Conflicts

Community conflict can be classified into two categories: structural and interpersonal.

- Structural conflict is entirely avoidable: it arises from disagreements in how the community should work that haven't been property sorted out.

- Interpersonal conflict is trickier – we're all imperfect humans with different journeys and histories. Sometimes we're going to have different ways we approach things which will cause tensions with each other.

Structural conflict is conflict inherent in how a community is set up. It's entirely unnecessary and should be sorted out proactively and early. The best time to sort out structural conflict is before the community moves in. If it is sorted out in advance, it is resolved before it even becomes an issue. If you try to address structural conflict later on, it can be more difficult, more emotionally burdensome and sometimes prove intractable.

In our house we have a clear agreement. We wanted our commitment to each other to be substantive but fairly untaxing. There are four primary things that we expect from each other and hold each other to account over:

1 We each cook for the group one night a week;

2 We each clean for 30 minutes a week (rota tasks rotate);

3 Monday and Thursday at 7.30am we meditate for ½ hour together;

4 Sunday 7-9:30pm we eat and spend time together.

Everything beyond this agreed and expected list is considered "freely given" in our household. If someone decides to bake a cake, host friends, or take care of the garden, they do so out of their own free will and we are not obligated to help. This allows us to relax in our home in our own freedom, and for their gift to be a true gift (without expectations or strings attached).

Cleaning

Week ending Mon:	6 Feb	13 Feb	20 Feb	27 Feb	6 Mar	13 Mr
Food & Kitchen	N	T	B	A	R	G
Special Ops	G	N	T	B	A	R
Floor & Bins	R	G	N	T	B	A
Bathroom		A	R	G	N	T	B
Rest / Away	B / T	A / B	R / A	G / R	N / G	T / N

We have a simple cleaning rota on the chalkboard which is ticked off each week. One of the tasks is called 'Special Operations' – a wildcard task that you can invent for yourself (a deep clean, a repair, or creatively supporting the house or community to be more beautiful in some way). The rota has a couple of rest/away slots each week, and people can swap with each other to fit their schedules. We try to cycle our whole community through all the jobs, as we have found it helps us to all feel ownership and take care of the whole household.

It's crucial to have a clear understanding of the required commitment before joining an intentional community, as expectations can vary. Some may expect to spend time together every night, while others may be out most nights. Either way may be acceptable, but it's important to know beforehand.

When recruiting new community members, an agreement both helps in setting expectations before they move in, and for inducting them in the first weeks. Maybe the first generation of "pioneers" have a good understanding of what the vision and agreements are, but how can this be shared with a new person who moves in a few years down the line? Our house has an agreement that outlines the shared vision, commitments, and expectations of the community members. The house agreement is a "living document" that is updated occasionally as the community evolves (we used Google Docs).

A written agreement is vital to protect the community: if at some point you have someone in the community who is living divergently from the agreement, it is much easier (and less personal) to address it by referring to an impartial written agreement that has set out clear expectations. The conversation then moves from "I don't like how you're behaving", to become "is there something we can do to help you meet this agreement, does the agreement need to change, or is this still how you want to live?"

After 10 years, we have taken it to the nth degree: For each of the weekly cleaning tasks we have a laminated bullet point list clearly stating what each task involves. This seems pedantic at first, but avoids a huge number of potential minor conflicts and potential for subtle resentments, which are toxic to community life.

Structural conflict can often be avoided through clear planning and documentation. We have created community agreements with many of the communities I have lived in and they have served us well. An example is included at the end of this chapter for reference and inspiration. While it may seem detailed, each bullet point represents a future conflict or misunderstanding avoided. For example, if you write down in advance how people can safely move out and how new community members will be chosen, it minimises the risk of later friction or dispute.

No agreement is ever going to solve everything. Indeed there is a danger of things becoming bureaucratic. A rule of thumb for systems – and one of the many quotes attributed to Einstein – is to keep systems "as simple as possible, but no simpler". Where we lack self-awareness in how we navigate our lives together, we will still have interpersonal conflict, discussed on the following page in section 4.

Types of space

There are several types of spaces that communities can meet in. It's important to be clear on the differences between them:

- Heart-oriented spaces are spaces primarily for listening to each other, and empathising with each other. In the communities that I have been in we have tried to not to interrupt or be right in these spaces, just to listen deeply. Often we will each take it in turns to speak, not responding directly to each other or trying to persuade each other, but rather each sharing from our own experience;

- Decision-oriented spaces are spaces aimed at making effective decisions. In these spaces we engage in constructive dialogue. We may choose to use hand signals and to organise with minutes and agendas. In the communities I have been a part of we have generally tried to use consensus for setting overall direction, and then have delegated the details.

A few tips that we have found useful:

- Differentiate between heart- and decision-oriented spaces both in time and location. If you can, go so far as to have them in different locations (the kitchen vs. the living room). Be careful not to let your weekly emotional check-in blend with your monthly house practicalities meeting;

- Always have meetings after a meal when people are well fed. Decisions tend to be smoother on a full stomach;

- Schedule meetings for regular slots (e.g. weekly on a Wednesday, or first Thursday of the month). This avoids a lot of time comparing diaries;

- Give pre-permission for people to miss things 20% of the time as long as they message to apologise. This saves a lot of resentment, means that you aren't constantly rescheduling to meet people's varying needs, and that people have automatic permission to feel too tired on occasion.

4. Turn towards and learn skills to enable you to grow as a result of Interpersonal Conflicts

Communities should take time in their early months to learn ways to deal with interpersonal conflicts peacefully. This takes practice: Nonviolent *Communication* by Marshall B. Rosenberg is a great tool that communities can learn to use together as a group. I'd highly recommend training yourselves in the use of this as a community before major conflict arises.

When a conflict arises, there is a choice: (a) you can turn towards it, or (b) you can avoid it. If you avoid conflicts, even the small ones, then at best the relationship becomes stale in that particular area and starts to 'crust over'. This can lead to a gradual withering and slow decline of the individual relationship, and damage the community fabric. If you want to grow as a community, then you'll see that there really is only one option: (a). The key to interpersonal conflict is for everyone in the community to be committed to turning towards it, seeing it as an opportunity for personal growth, and learning the tools required to navigate it together.

If you proactively embrace the personal growth journey as one of your reasons for living together in community, it's going to greatly increase the chance of the community being successful. Through turning towards conflicts, and dealing with them in an effective and peaceful way, relationships may deepen beyond what you at first hoped was even possible. And you're going to grow as a person.

Have enough good times in the bank

Having regular, positive experiences with your community members can make addressing conflicts much easier. It's important to have a strong foundation of good times and positive interactions with others in the community. This can help create a comfortable and relaxed environment when addressing any problems that arise. Bringing up a minor issue feels much easier if you've just had a great time with someone the night before.

A housemate and I once realised that too much negativity was affecting our interactions. We decided to start going for a weekly walk together around the local park. This simple act helped add enough positivity to our relationship and reduced the small conflicts we were facing. If you are feeling difficulties start to emerge with a community member, ask yourself: when was the last time you did something joyful with them?

Generosity of spirit

Some interpersonal conflicts may exist because of subtle philosophical differences, neither 'right' nor 'wrong'. If one person's approach to the cleaning is to do the minimum stipulated, because their philosophy of life is about keeping 'work' efficiently minimised, while another's personal philosophy is about doing things to the best of their ability or lovingly tending to their home, then this may create subtle conflict unless it is consciously unpacked and addressed.

It is often easier to see the work that we do ourselves, than to see work that others are doing. Sometimes I forget that a particular task exists if it's always done by someone else (e.g. paying a bill, or cleaning a particular thing). I have found it helps me to be more generous if I periodically try to recognise all the work that is being done (emotional and practical) that I have not done recently. It helps hugely if I trust the intentions of the people I'm living with, regardless of how talented they are at a particular household task.

The problem of "givers and takers" is as relevant to intentional communities as it is in wider society. Deeper living together in community is also about a paradigm shift in how we see the world. Rules will only get us so far. Are we just responsible for ourselves, or also for each other? Do I treat you as I would want to be treated? Is your happiness also my happiness? Can we stop seeing the world simply from an individualistic perspective? If we move from 'me to we' together, then can we co-create a new paradigm for living together?

When times are tough

Community building requires patience. I have found that a community's underlying mood often follows a seasonal pattern that is better measured in months rather than weeks. During an initial "honeymoon" phase, which I have found often lasts for around six months, it can be challenging to envision the "winter" of disillusionment that may follow when the community is no longer new and exciting, and conflicts start to arise. Conversely, during a frustrating season that lasts several months, it can be challenging to imagine the harmonious season that could come next.

In times of struggle, it can be tempting to abandon a community altogether. While there are instances where it may be the wisest choice to exit in the most responsible way possible, it's also worth considering reinvesting just when others are starting to give up.

Reinvesting just when others are starting to give up can sometimes be an inspiring, visionary, courageous, wise and resource-effective thing to do. One or two people can have a ripple effect and make all the difference. Understanding that communities can have natural long-wavelength fluctuations, can help avoid despair and encourage reinvestment of patience, love, intention, and effort during the community's "winter" when things seem most bleak.

In many ways it seems a lot like gardening. Growth is measured in seasons. We don't harvest in the same season that we plant – it's more like 6 months later. If our tree of a community has wilted or is diseased, is the best course to give up and make space for something new, or is it best to prune it, water it and be patient? It is unlikely that we will witness all the good that may come from the plants and seeds that we nurture. Some will be subtle and unseen, or enjoyed by people yet to come.

High demand

My experience of creating intentional urban communities in London over the past decade has been that there is an incredibly high demand for healthy residential communities. In the past, when advertising for a spare room in our intentional community, we have often received over 100 responses within a short period of time. While this demand may not be as pronounced in smaller cities, if you create a healthy rented urban community there is generally more demand than supply. This has often enabled us to find very aligned new community members (in one case creating a successful rented community in an empty house from an advert in just a month, with a thorough process!). Do not worry too much if you end up with an extra room or two when looking for a property in a city with a busy rental market – you can probably fill it.

When advertising community spaces, we utilised multiple platforms, including social media, Facebook groups, the Spareroom website, and direct shout-outs to friendship networks through email, WhatsApp, and Signal.

To streamline the selection process and ensure that applicants had fully read the advertisement, we requested that they write a short statement of around 150 words on why they would be a good fit for the community. Approximately half of applicants took the time to do this, which saved us (and them) a huge amount of time in to-and-fro conversations. We used a Google Spreadsheet to summarise the responses received each week and used this to ask community members which people they thought might make a good fit (we had a pre-discussion around appropriate criteria and removed names and ages from the sheet to minimise unconscious biases).

One of our priorities was to be respectful to people who had applied to live with us – avoiding causing unnecessary disappointment or wasting their time. For example, instead of inviting a large number of people to meet the community in person, we only invited a small number who we felt would be a realistic fit after an initial video call.

Final Thought

Communities are complex webs of relationships. If intentional community living isn't for you right now, I hope that by consciously unpacking what helps communities to thrive, you come across something valuable that will support the relationships and communities in your own life.

And if intentional community living is for you: Can you find a group of aligned people who are willing to embark on the journey? Go away together. Consider renting before buying, even if a permanent property is on the cards. Don't wait for the perfect forever-property before you start living in community. Put the people before the property.

Appendix: Example Intentional Community Agreement

Our community agreements have served us well for the communities that I have lived in. Different communities will require different agreements. In this instance, ours was simplified by not being intergenerational and not having any members with additional support needs. While it may seem detailed, each bullet point represents a future conflict or misunderstanding avoided.

Shared Meals

- We share all our food, so anyone can eat anything in the kitchen unless it is clearly labelled otherwise. We use bags to indicate the occasional food items that are not for communal consumption (e.g. tupperware with tomorrow's lunch? Put it in a bag inside the fridge).

- We aim to cook for the house at least once a week on average. This could be preparing food to go in the fridge that others can eat when they feel like it, or cooking lunch/dinner for everyone who is in. We use the house noticeboard in the kitchen to indicate each week which nights we are in and when we are cooking. Dinner is cooked for 7pm.

- We take it in turns to wash up after communal meals. If you cooked, you are responsible for cleaning the food preparation area and equipment used to prepare food. You don't have to wash up the dishes the food was served on.

- We aim to cook a fairly large amount, ideally so that there are leftovers for people coming home late and for lunch the next day.

- The house is strictly vegetarian. No meat or fish can be cooked in the kitchen without prior agreement of the whole house. Communal meals should be vegan-friendly.

- We tend to eat organic and fairtrade where possible and lean towards pretty healthy food.

Collective Responsibility

- We take collective responsibility for the care of the house, and try to keep it tidy for each other.

For example, when we finish in the kitchen, we try to wash up the things we have used.

- We sit down for a house meeting roughly once a month to check in with each other. We try to use this as an opportunity to bring any issues or concerns up before they get too big, and encourage each other to do this in an honest and kind way.

- The expectation is that everyone will do the following things on average once each week:

- We each cook for the group one night a week.

- We each clean for 30 minutes a week (rota tasks rotate).

- Monday & Thursday at 7.30am we meditate for ½ an hour together

- Sunday 7-9:30pm we eat and spend time together.

Excerpt from the cleaning rota. Over time it can easily cause resentment if people have different ideas of what a cleaning task means.

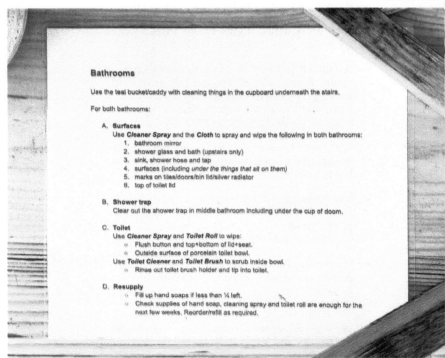

Bathrooms

Use the teal bucket/caddy with cleaning things in the cupboard underneath the stairs.

For both bathrooms:

A. **Surfaces**
   Use *Cleaner Spray* and the *Cloth* to spray and wipe the following in both bathrooms:
   1. bathroom mirror
   2. shower glass and bath (upstairs only)
   3. sink, shower hose and tap
   4. surfaces (including *under the things that sit on them*)
   5. marks on tiles/doors/bin lid/silver radiator
   6. top of toilet lid

B. **Shower trap**
   Clear out the shower trap in middle bathroom including under the cup of doom.

C. **Toilet**
   Use *Cleaner Spray* and *Toilet Roll* to wipe:
   o Flush button and top+bottom of lid+seat.
   o Outside surface of porcelain toilet bowl.
   Use *Toilet Cleaner* and *Toilet Brush* to scrub inside bowl.
   o Rinse out toilet brush holder and tip into toilet.

D. **Resupply**
   o Fill up hand soaps if less than ¼ left.
   o Check supplies of hand soap, cleaning spray and toilet roll are enough for the next few weeks. Reorder/refill as required.

- Any time put into the house in addition to the above is freely given. For example, if some of us choose to work on the garden, spend time hosting guests, or bake a cake, we take care not to feel resentment towards anyone who is not choosing to do this, or believe that they are somehow 'not doing their fair share'.

- We have a cleaning rota, and each spend about 30 mins a week cleaning (hoovering, bathrooms, kitchen etc.). We aim to clean on Sundays (or one day either side).

- As a community we try to minimise our impact on the planet. This means taking responsibility for small things like minimising energy, food & other waste; and also welcoming initiatives in this area.

Sex and Relationships

- Sex in individual bedrooms only, not in communal spaces.

- All genders, orientations and relationship constellations are welcome.

- We are free to bring sexual partners to the house, with the intention of being respectful to housemates and to maintaining a peaceful atmosphere. Given that we are living in a communal space, we try to be considerate of how people we invite over might place a social burden on others while using the communal areas.

- We trust each other to choose relationships that are right for us, and partners are welcome to stay over for a few nights. If a partner stays over most nights for more than a two weeks, then this should be discussed at a community meeting to check whether it's ok.

- If a partner stays over most nights for more than a week, then they may be asked to contribute their share of the collective food and bills. If someone ends up staying more than a month, then typically the rental cost of the room will be increased (with a corresponding reduction to the cost of the other rooms).

Money and Shared Resources

- We share the following items which are paid for communally: cleaning supplies, washing liquid, basic bathroom supplies, bills and food. We aim to live in a spirit of trust and friendship, and keep things simple, so we all pay the same amount.

- Note that shared expenses exclude meals out, takeaways and alcohol.

- We aim to lean towards organic and fairtrade food, and ecological cleaning supplies where possible. We sometimes purchase bulk supplies from a co-operative wholesaler such as Suma/Infinity.

- Items are paid for from each of our own finances and then the cost is reimbursed by other community members. We use a simple online tool (e.g. Splitwise) to keep track of how much we owe each other. We aim to not be more than £150 in debt to other community members at any time.

Guests and Events

- Guests are welcome, especially partners and family members, to come over for dinner or overnight. We intend to message/email in advance to let each other know and check it's ok for guests to come.

- We recognise the need to keep our community fresh, and offer a genuine welcome to visitors. We are mindful to not overextend ourselves if we do not have sufficient energy between us to welcome people.

- We intend to use the spaces in our house to occasionally host groups from the wider community (e.g. a gong bath in the living room). While only some of us may be involved in organising a particular group, we all intend to be welcoming to the space being used in this way occasionally.

- Guests who are staying for a week or more are expected to help out with the cooking, cleaning and washing up.

- Guests who are staying for 2 weeks or more should be considered at a house meeting.

Moving In and Moving Out

- We intend to live in the house for at least a year, conditions permitting.

- We give at least the following notice of the exact date we intend to move out. We aim to give as much notice as possible, with a minimum of 6 weeks (ideally 10 weeks).

- Any community member staying in a double room is liable for the whole cost of the room if their partner moves out and they choose to remain, unless a reduction is agreed by the other community members.

- Unless otherwise agreed, new community members will be decided by the following process:

- advertise the room online and through friendship networks

- use a name/age-hidden spreadsheet and pre-discussed criteria to create shortlist based on 150 word responses

- interview a shortlist of candidates (use video-calls for initial interviews if it's a long list)

- the remaining community members choose new member

Subletting

- Subletting is ok if a suitable person is found and agreed mutually with the remaining community members. The person who is going away is liable for any shortfall in rent, food and bills due to any gaps in occupancy. It is their responsibility to initiate the search for a subletter.

- If one of us is away for more than 3 months, then it is considered that we have effectively moved out and we lose our right to automatically move back. This is because we want to be fair to whoever currently lives in the community, and not give founding members special priority.

Alcohol and Other

- Alcohol is fine in the house, as long as it is usually consumed responsibly so that people are still able to be aware and sensitive towards others.

- Care should be taken to not disrupt the peaceful atmosphere of the house, if occasionally taking intoxicating substances.

- Where possible, we aim to let the group know what we are up to, so that we can have open communication, take care of each other and know what to do in emergencies.

Noah Walton
has been setting up small intentional communities in London over the past 10 years. He is the founder of Eco Soul, a not-for-profit in London seeking to offer overnight guest accommodation alongside plant-based communal meals, social change talks and community workshops. He offers workshops to support new intentional communities. noah@ecosoullondon.com

The Growth of Urban Cohousing in the UK

MARTIN FIELD

Thanks to the determination of cohousing groups, urban cohousing has been gathering momentum. This article gives an overview of the schemes now established in UK towns and cities.

Within his earlier piece in this book, Blase Lambert notes how people from a wide range of backgrounds are looking to create different kinds of futures from those they most routinely experience:

"... students that don't want to be exploited by the financialisation of halls of residence, young people who want an alternative to unaffordable home ownership or overpriced private renting, groups of older people who want an alternative to a traditional care home, multi-generational groups that want to live in a mutually supportive environment or people who want to create a better and more sustainable future; the emergence of community land trusts, cohousing communities, mutual home ownership societies, student housing co-operatives and new forms of collective ownership."

There is a strong communal theme running through these scenarios, a strong sense of 'groups' interested in ways that people could support each other and find more than just a secure and reliable roof over one's head. Many contemporary collaborative housing projects in the UK demonstrate a strong commitment to finding alternatives to the speculative and acquisitive nature of the mainstream 'housing market' – such as by establishing the long-term affordability of local accommodation costs, or by improving the utility and performance of existing (and often neglected) housing stock in order to maximise efficiencies and reduce energy consumption. As this writer has noted elsewhere,[1] there are a variety of collaborative 'models' used in the UK (also recorded by the 'Community Led Homes' network)[2] that function as the different means to combine and focus collective energies and resources, although some care is needed to understand what people are seeking as the final outcomes from their joined endeavours and of what kind of endeavours could best shape the future to fit with their ideals. For some projects, however, the core intention is to create more than just good dwellings, more than just an efficient family home for a private household, but also for a more embracive and social setting to provide residents with the opportunities and spaces to mix and share local things together in their daily and local lives. It is an intention for a more mutually shared lifestyle, rather than remaining forever separated in the 'nucleated' dwellings that are the mainstay of mainstream housing provision.

What follows below is a focus on a particular approach to realising such ends – the 'cohousing' ideal, where neighbours deliberately craft together a mix of private and communal facilities that link residences with other shared and communal space, all within a deliberate ethos of creating an 'intentional neighbourhood' for a supportive and shared life, in common with others having similar values.

The use or notion of the 'cohousing' concept needs some careful deliberation here. There has been an unhelpful habit by some commentators to bracket a wide variety of collaborative endeavours with the label of being 'co-housing' [see [3]]. This becomes quite unhelpful when examining what is evidently innovative in the kinds of cohousing settings from Scandinavia or North America that are routinely quoted as the character of shared neighbourhoods that UK projects wish to emulate. Not all collaborative schemes are 'cohousing' ones – a degree of shared activity in their creation is not sufficient in itself to warrant that description, just as not all projects that function in a co-operative fashion will create, or are designed to function as, formal housing 'co-ops'. What does distinguish the fundamental values of cohousing

1   "Creating Community-Led and Self-Build Homes: a guide to collaborative practice in the UK", (M Field) Policy Press, 2020.

2   See: communityledhomes.org.uk

3   Unhelpful, in that a number of commentators have used the word with a hyphen as synonymous with projects that are generally collaborative in their nature, or have some element of shared provisions, thereby detracting from the term 'cohousing' denoting solely the combination of characteristics described in the text here.

projects is altogether more tangible: as the newly published *UKCN Practical Guide to Cohousing* (produced for the UK Cohousing Network)[4] spells out, the core criteria for identifying a verifiable 'cohousing' project will be those projects which have:

- decisions taken under the control of the prospective residents – it is the group that manages and is responsible for overseeing the co-design, co-development and co-organisation of the shared neighbourhood;

- a design of the physical form and layout of the neighbourhoods to maximise incidental and organised contact between residents;

- self-contained accommodation, plus significant common facilities and spaces, of which a 'common house' is a crucial setting for communal activities where the common facilities operate as shared extensions to private dwellings and their amenities;

- an appropriate size and scale of each neighbourhood setting to underpin the sustainable community dynamics in that neighbourhood and for meaningful relationships to develop between its households.

In other words, at the heart of the success of the classic cohousing projects that continue to inspire so many new projects, lies a fundamental accountability and control of the future neighbourhood back to a clear decision-making by the future residents, coupled with appropriate designs for supporting the size, dynamics and dimensions of how private and communal places can combine to underpin a sustainable sociability.

Taken individually, each of the above criteria might seem analogous to the motivations behind other collaborative or communal intents – such as the collective decision-making behind the inspiring Ashley Vale[5] self-build neighbourhood in Bristol, or the modern dwelling units and shared facilities designed by housing association projects to support elderly citizens. On closer scrutiny, however, the character and vivacity of cohousing places provides very tangible evidence of

"The UKCN Practical Guide to Cohousing", (ed. M Field et al) Diggers & Dreamers Publications, 2022.

See: Ashley Vale Action Group community self build. – The Self Build Guide (www.the-self-build-guide.co.uk/ashley-vale-action-group/)

what the necessary combination of the above criteria can create: the practical outcomes of cohousing projects are manifest in how its comprehensive 'participatory process' steers the neighbourhood's form and facilities to maximise the creation of a shared identity and a supportive neighbourhood life. As McCamant and Durrett, the immensely influential promoters of cohousing outside of its Scandinavian background, have noted:

"none of these characteristics is unique [to cohousing], but the consistent combination of all four is…".[6]

Summarising the more theoretical background to cohousing aspirations is one thing – bringing UK projects into reality is certainly another. Whilst there remains a widespread and continual interest in replicating the creation of such 'intentional' neighbourhoods, the relatively small number of realised projects in the UK is one consequence of the practical obstacles to embarking on such a provision that is outside of the usual formats for how places and dwellings are designed and delivered – usually by large scale housebuilders or property developers, with little appetite or patience for building 'from the bottom up'. The very nature of harnessing the separate energies of future residents and the financial resources they might access with land and support from mainstream partners or regulators has often proved to be extremely convoluted. When faced with the sustained challenges and opposition from external bodies whose established interests are primarily wedded to perpetuating their own opportunities within the status quo, some groups have simply not been able to pull the necessary elements of a successful development together.

Of the UK cohousing projects that have nevertheless steered a path through such challenging scenarios, their combined successes show both a variety of settings and a range of local motivations – rural and urban; new-build and retrofit; inter-generational and those more for 'senior' residents. The range and combination of these scenarios also reflects how cohousing ideals are being applied creatively to the development opportunities that are available 'on-the-ground', if the possibility of acquiring an ideal greenfield site is not forthcoming.

For deliberate purposes, the following commentary is solely focused upon cohousing projects that have

---

6   "Creating Cohousing – Building Sustainable Communities" (K McCamant and C Durrett), New Society Publishers, 2011 p.43

emerged and have been established in UK urban areas,[7] principally over the past twenty-five years: it should be noted, however, that issues raised along the way are ones that may challenge the development of UK projects in both urban and rural settings alike.

Following the pioneering work of the recognisably modern cohousing projects at Laughton Lodge outside Lewes, and at Frankleigh House outside Bradford on Avon,[8] both of which made innovative use of existing buildings, the first deliberate newbuild cohousing project was the Springhill community scheme located at the side of the town centre in Stroud. This benefited from the site being purchased by one of the core members before a group was properly in place, but with the key intention of it being the basis for a group-led cohousing initiative that would attract other households. The intention was always to create accommodation for a mix of households, families and ages, with all the other desired facilities that would support communal interactions.

Example: Springhill, Stroud, Gloucestershire

Dwellings
34 units, primarily houses and a few flats

Other facilities
common house; lounge and meeting rooms

Key elements
newbuild; 'intergenerational'

Date of first occupants
2003

Tenure and ownership
group freehold of land, dwellings are leasehold ownership

Source of land
purchase on the 'open market'

Website
www.springhillcohousing.com

---

[7]   To be clear, the discussion from this point does not consider rural or semi-rural cohousing settings such as Thundercliffe Grange; Canon Frome; the Threshold Centre; East Whins at Findhorn; or Laughton Lodge: details of all can be found on the UKCN website: cohousing.org.uk

[8]   See also UKCN website: cohousing.org.uk

Springhill's member households collectively became the freeholder of the site, and commissioned all the design, construction and other professional arrangements for financing the scheme and moving into the leasehold-based dwellings on completion. For many of the original households, this move into the cohousing community required the prior sale of the property they had previously inhabited, and a subsequent transfer of mortgage or other loan finance arrangements.

Example: Forgebank, Halton, Lancashire

Dwellings
41 units, primarily houses plus a few flats

Other facilities
Common House; guest rooms; laundry; workshops and offices

Key elements
newbuild; inter-generational

Date of first occupants
2012

Tenure and ownership
group freehold of land; dwellings are leasehold ownership

Source of land
purchase on the 'open market'

Website
www.lancastercohousing.org.uk

This format for how a contemporary group of initially disparate households could collectively form and shape a new cohousing neighbourhood was adopted by people in the Lancaster area, also looking at creating an inter-generational setting for a mix of families and ages. After some extensive searching for a feasible and affordable site, a location was found by the riverside at Halton to one side of Lancaster city, where a site had been approved for newbuild housing development, but an original developer's financial distress enabled the group to acquire the land on viable terms.

The Halton site (since named Forgebank) also included a three-storey disused mill building that would require renovation by the formal planning permission. The availability of its spaces and facilities has subsequently provided many opportunities to integrate the cohousing community and its setting into the surrounding local networks, and to enable others to see a modern 'collective' life in operation!

Whilst this freeholder-leaseholder format was evidencing one means for how new schemes might be delivered by group-led activity, there developed a growing awareness that the practical realisation of such approaches could well become quite exclusive, being only really available to households that already had use of private financial resources or some other property asset (even if that was just an existing mortgage) that could fund a household's move into this kind of cohousing. What was not yet evident was the means for how groups that included member households with more modest levels of resources (including benefit-level incomes) might complete a cohousing development that could genuinely include people from a range of incomes, family make-ups, and financial backgrounds.

The 'mutual ownership' scheme devised for LILAC[9] in Leeds – the 'Low Impact Living Affordable Community' – subsequently developed one particular response to this challenge together with a focus on eco-sensitive designs and construction) on a tight urban site that was purchased in negotiation from Leeds City Council. This was the creation of a co-operative approach that enabled a group's members to be participating in cohousing development that would accord with their own personal incomes or resources, as well as enabling the development and operational costs of the overall cohousing initiative to still be achievable as a whole. This 'mutual ownership' model included mechanisms for what levels of contribution each member would make, as a percentage of their regular incomes; collective and perpetual ownership of the properties and facilities that were created; and a further mechanism for calculating what kind of 'equity'-based figure any individual co-operative member might receive, if the household wished to move away from the neighbourhood at a future date.

9   With support from the Confederation of Co-operative Housing (CCH), and the subsequent registration of a further set of Model Rules by CCH (see: cch.coop/registered-model-rules/).

Example:
LILAC, Leeds

Dwellings
20 units, a mix of houses plus apartments

Other facilities
Common House; allotments and play areas

Key elements
inter-generational; eco-build; innovative mutual finance

Date of first occupants
2013

Tenure and ownership
mutual home ownership society

Source of land
former school site, purchased from Leeds City Council'

Website
www.lilac.coop

The LILAC (short for Low Impact Living Affordable Community) project has been hugely respected for its innovative approach in creating the opportunity for a range of households with a diverse mix of economic resources to collaborate within a combined scheme. It is also shown how a collective neighbourhood scheme can use a mutual and shared ownership model to retain its properties' values as a whole, and not see this swallowed up by a speculative gain to individual households – a complaint raised against some cohousing schemes elsewhere the terms of individual leasehold ownership has been a factor in subsequent sales at 'open market' values further limiting who may have the finances to buy into that community setting in the future. There has accordingly been strong interest in being able to replicate other 'mutual home ownership' schemes elsewhere, such as the planning approval now obtained for the cohousing project at Lowfield Green[10] within the broader YorSpace[11] area development in York.

Chapeltown Cohousing (ChaCo) in action

Other practical support to a cohousing project from Leeds City Council has been in providing a site for the long awaited Chapeltown Cohousing project, along with providing an element of its development funds in the form of loan finance from the Public Works Loan Board, an extremely invaluable source of funds at low interest rates[12]. Mindful that some criticism of cohousing projects is for seeming predominantly 'middle-class' in style and based in areas with little diversity in their household make-up, the Chapeltown scheme – 'ChaCo' – has sprung from a very diverse and multi-ethnic area of Leeds and has sought to create a cohousing setting that honestly reflects the range of ethnicities and social backgrounds present in the area.

10 See: yorspace.org

11 Note the case study: communityledhomes.org.uk/resource/mutual-home-ownership-high-value-area

12 This is the only cohousing scheme to date that has secured such PWLB support.

Example: Chapeltown Cohousing, Leeds

Dwellings
33 units, a mix of houses and flats

Other facilities
common house; guest rooms; laundry, workshop

Key elements
newbuild; diversity & inclusion; low carbon footprint

Date of first occupants
2022

Tenure and ownership
group freehold of land; dwellings are leasehold ownership, shared-ownership and rent

Source of land
acquired from Leeds City Council

Website
www.chapeltowncohousing.org.uk

Another of the factors that enabled the ChaCo group to finally build on the land allocated to them was sharing the development of their site with a local housing association[13], which would develop more traditional units for itself; plus the allocation of four plots for self-build housing units in the future.

All the schemes noted above have been focused on accommodating a spread of households and ages, drawing inspiration from the inter-generational settings that had featured in the engaging publicity and information on established cohousing neighbourhoods in Scandinavia, Europe and North America. It has been evident, however, that some initiatives abroad showed community settings deliberately geared towards supportive neighbourhood settings that were primarily for older citizens (usually in age from 50+), as distinct from accommodating broader family-backgrounds

"offering a realistic alternative to a tradition of paternalism and benign neglect of the old... [thereby] involving the older person as citizen not service recipient"[14].

In looking to craft similar kinds of age-specific schemes in the UK, it took many years of raising such possibilities in policy and development sector debates, and a significant willingness by formal partners to provide financial assistance and expertise, before a pioneering group of women from across London (Older Women in Cohousing, OWCH) was finally able to secure their site in Barnet as the first such 'senior' setting, in this case for women aged over 50.

The 'New Ground' newbuild scheme, with its street-fronted facades carefully inserted around grounds formally used for a religious establishment, has rightly won a host of national and international design awards for meeting all its aims so inspirationally. Careful consideration was given to making its internal and external environments barrier-free, evident in its ground-floor siting of the main common areas and its left access to all floors. The scheme is rightly signposting what further 'senior' UK schemes can achieve, both for single and for mixed-gender occupation.

---

13 Unity Housing

14 See: housinglin.org.uk/Topics/browse/Housing/HousingforOlderPeople/Cohousing/

Example: New Ground, Barnet, London

Dwellings
25 flats

Other facilities
common room (catering, etc.); guest rooms; laundry

Key elements
newbuild; focus on 'senior' residents (50+)

Date of first occupants
2016

Tenure and ownership
group freehold of land; dwellings are leasehold ownership and rent

Source of land
acquired by and from Housing Association partner

Website
www.newgroundcohousing.uk

One example of a subsequent mixed-gender development has been the newbuild scheme at Cannock Mill in Essex. This has again been developed for people over fifty, mainly and originally also from the broader North London area, who could not find a suitable site closer to their existing homes, and who subsequently agreed to relocate en masse to an urban area of Colchester.

Example: Cannock Mill, Colchester, Essex

Dwellings
23 units, mainly houses plus some flats (plus 3 flats to come)

Other facilities
retrofit + newbuild; 'senior' focus; 'passive' eco-design

Key elements
newbuild; inter-generational

Date of first occupants
2019

Tenure and ownership
group freehold of land; dwellings are leasehold ownership

Source of land
purchase on the 'open market'

Website
www.cannockmillcohousing.co.uk

This site came with its challenges, not least a large pre-existing timber-frame mill building that would require retention (which has subsequently become a striking setting for the 'common house' and other shared facilities) and a significantly sloping site that ultimately required some flexibility to core design principles of trying to keep vehicle movements to the edge of a site. Despite these challenges, the purchase price for the site was still high (which may have been a factor in why it had not been already purchased by mainstream property developers) and the group needed to acknowledge that a scheme would be achievable overall but would limit initial participation by households without sufficient finances to meet all the costs of final occupation.[15]

---

15 There are plans for an additional renovation of a previous but unused office building on the site that could provide 'affordable' tenures in the future.

In hoping to navigate their ways around the worst of the UK's property market and its ever-rising prices for anything to buy or on which to build, some groups have looked to the public sector for support in securing a viable cohousing site on which to house local people. Substantial pockets of land are still held by public sector bodies, and it is possible that some of their sites could be ones on which a cohousing project might be established, although securing sufficient local political support to acquire any of its land could take some extended time. A degree of caution is also required for how any aspirations for a 'self-commissioned' project are perceived by some local authority contacts, as the public sector's role in housing people 'in the greatest need' can still evoke paternalistic patterns of response in which the fundamental basis of group-led solutions may not fit! Even where local authorities are willing to release some land for 'community-led' proposals, cohousing groups may need to ensure that core members are not identified as somehow ineligible for occupation of the properties created[16], or that the site does not come burdened with such requirements that would seriously comprise its future operation as a self-managed neighbourhood.

Given the typical frameworks in which land and sites are bought and traded in the UK (supported by policy pressures on public sector bodies to raise as much finance as possible through transactions at open market norms) many substantial parcels of land identified for future residential development are already in the ownership (or under some pre-purchase control) of mainstream developer and housebuilding interests and await the commencement of on-site developments at some future date. Groups looking for land of a size suitable for the development of a cohousing project may therefore need to consider how to promote their use of one piece of land within a wider development zone. The principle of inserting a potential opportunity for a collective or communal endeavour (like cohousing) within a wider development plan could itself be something that a local authority is asked to support.

One recent example of including some land in a wider programme of development sites for a collective or collaborative outcome has been the Marmalade Lane neighbourhood scheme, within the broader area development of Orchard Park in the northern part of Cambridge. Longstanding lobbying of the local author-

16 See the 'Group' sections on working with external partners in the "The UKCN Practical Guide to Cohousing", op cit.

ity sector by cohousing enthusiasts over many years had not met with much success until a site was earmarked for a particular kind of 'developer-enabled' project, where this could support aspiring households to work collectively and create a cohousing result. The local authority shaped the basic planning requirements[17] under which the site would need to be designed and developed and appointed a private sector developer to work with the subsequent cohousing group, put the detailed proposals together and commission the eventual construction.

Example: Marmalade Lane Cambridge

Dwellings
42 units, a mix of houses and apartments

Other facilities
common house; gym; workshop; laundry; playrooms

Key elements
newbuild; inter-generational; 'passive' energy design

Date of first occupants
2018

Tenure and ownership
group freehold of land; dwellings are leasehold ownership

Source of land
purchase enabled via Cambridge City Council

Website
www.marmaladelane.co.uk

The outcome has been a clearly recognisable cohousing neighbourhood that is markedly distinct from the more mundane surrounding areas of then other new developments built through more mainstream housebuilding practice. The original design parameters stipulated by the local authority have, however, resulted in a large scheme, decidedly larger than what conventional cohousing 'wisdom' has seen as the preferred maximum number of adults,[18] if the development of a close inter-neighbourly cohousing

7   In this instance, it was the local authority which agreed at the start that the site would not need to provide units for 'affordable housing'.

8   Being a range of between 20-50 adults, plus children: see "Creating Cohousing – Building Sustainable Communities"; and "Creating Community-Led and Self-Build Homes", both op cit

dynamic is not to be disadvantaged. It may take some time before larger UK sites that are being considered for potential cohousing development are confident in building more than one self-contained neighbourhood, even on adjacent plots!

Looking to include an opportunity for a new cohousing development into wider area proposals is also the basis for another senior cohousing scheme currently in the development pipeline, namely the Still Green[19] project. This has secured planning approval for a complex of 29 apartments for over-fifties as part of the wider urban development now taking shape in the Wolverton area of Milton Keynes.

Yet not all current and past cohousing groups have been focused on securing a vacant site on which to build entirely new properties, and there has been a growing interest in obtaining existing urban buildings from which a cohousing neighbourhood could be modelled. The UK Cohousing Network call such an endeavour a 'retrofitting' of cohousing into the existing urban fabric, perhaps even by reconfiguring how an existing collection of dwellings could be given a revised and 'collective' identity.

One such 'retrofit' development has been undertaken by the 'On the Brink' community in the Nether Edge area of Sheffield. A large residential property (an early-Victorian urban villa) was jointly purchased by the members of the cohousing group. This has been redesigned internally to provide the core of the project's first units of accommodation and initial common areas,[20] and then to construct additional dwellings built onto the original house, via a deliberate expansion of the built footprint within the property's grounds.

The 'common' facilities here are therefore not located in a stand-alone new building, such as at Springhill or Forgebank, but have been modelled from spaces that were made available from within the internal footprint of the original house.

---

19 See: stillgreenweb.org
20 A similar approach to that taken many years before by Thundercliffe Grange in Rotherham.

Dwellings
19 units, primarily apartments plus a few houses

Other facilities
Communal spaces for cooking, eating, meetings

Key elements
retrofit + newbuild; 'intergenerational'.

Date of first occupants
2015

Tenure and ownership
group freehold; leasehold ownership

Source of land
purchase on the 'open market'

Website
www.onthebrink.community

Example:
On the Brink,
Sheffield

This overall range of cohousing settings provides very clear examples of what people are doing with cohousing ideals in urban areas, and what will continue to emerge if new projects, like in Bridport[21] and Norwich[22] and the Halton Senior Cohousing[23] project (drawing directly from the experience of the original Forgebank community just next door), are able to complete all the elements required for their schemes. There certainly exist more financing opportunities for new schemes than in previous times, and there are a range of social lenders who can be very supportive of projects and groups that are able to produce a credible business plan for how a new scheme can be viable. The availability of suitable urban land or sites is still more challenging, almost more than for those groups looking for a rural site on which to establish an 'off-grid' future! Given the general difficulties that many community projects experience in trying to acquire vacant housing development sites – difficulties due not least to their relative weakness in competing with mainstream developers and established property networks – it should be assumed that some future cohousing projects may be

---

21 See:bridportcohousing.org.uk/contact/
22 See: angelyard.org.uk
23 See: haltonseniorcohousing.org.uk

more successful at acquiring and remodelling an existing property instead, or (like Cannock Mill) be ready to look at sites that other developers have turned away from.

Some new groups are also looking at combining the cohousing ethos of support and communality with intentions to use this to meet other social ends, such as providing more modern supportive settings for households with vulnerable members (such as family members with learning impairments), or for the provision of specific support for people from less stable, even homeless, backgrounds. One such project is Graceworks Gardens[24] in Leicestershire, currently negotiating the purchase of a large property and grounds on which to develop a cohousing community with a strong commitment to helping homeless households, not least through past experience of generating horticultural training projects.

All new or aspiring projects will do well to consider what assistance they can glean from the experience that now exists within the UK's own Cohousing / Community-led sector – it is certainly no longer the case that valid expertise can only be imported from abroad. The experienced Facilitators with the regional Community Led Housing Hubs can steer new projects around their navigation of critical issues, and it will be sensible for projects to take seriously the employment of their own project manager, especially to help the development of appropriate liaisons and agreements with potential external partners, such as housing associations or property developers, and even with local authorities.

Lastly, various established cohousing communities and the UKCN provide regular training sessions to invite aspiring projects to hear of what projects did and didn't do to get their works completed, and the periodic 'UKCN newsletter' has become an invaluable source of up-to-date information.

The sector looks forward to hearing of the next successes!

---

24 See: graceworks.online

Dr Martin Field
has been a long-term advocate, researcher, practitioner and resident of community-led housing initiatives. He is currently employed by East Midlands Community Led Housing.

How to Set Up a Cohousing Community

DAVID MICHAEL

From first thoughts to moving in. David has founded four cohousing communities and this guide is based on his experiences of the disasters, headaches, regrets, learning and sometimes fun elements.

What is Cohousing and Why Do We Need It?

Cohousing consists of a pedestrianised housing complex, a common house used for regular meals, self contained units, no shared business or income, resident design input, and non-hierarchical and consensus decision making.

People need community and privacy. Cohousing is a way for people to live together so that they can have as much community and as much privacy as they want. The concept is simple and immediately comprehensible. It is the way forward for human beings, as social animals, to live together in a safe, independent and caring neighbourhood. It is a revolution that is beginning now. We will no longer just choose a new house when we move, we will join a new community.

How I Discovered Community Living and Cohousing

I first got excited by community when I read about socialism and kibbutz living in Israel. I visited and worked on a kibbutz in 1974 for a few months. It was a bit of a disappointment. I had read about the equality between men and women in the 1890s, working in the fields together and sharing in childcare. In my kibbutz, the men overwhelmingly worked on the land and women in the laundry, kitchen and childcare (though I know that many other kibbutzim did not divide roles so stereotypically). The volunteers were not integrated with the kibbutzniks (members) but rather formed their own volunteer community. Having said this, I did enjoy it overall, and that was where – as an 18 year old – I learnt to work hard and in the heat. I learnt that exerting myself and pushing through tiredness was more fun and felt great when I'd finished the day. I have carried that lesson through much of my life, including running up hills. I am essentially lazy and have to find methods for countering the "stop and rest" message. That can look like I'm keen and motivated.

So that experience left me not liking the rigidity of kibbutz. In 1994 I came upon the book, *Cohousing* by Kathryn Mcamant and Charles Durrett, who had coined the English word 'cohousing'. I had a flick through the book. I found cohousing easy to understand and I knew that's what I wanted to build. A year later my partner Helen and I bought a large mansion

in Wiltshire at auction, using £50,000 savings as a deposit. Four other mostly homeschooling families had committed to living there.

My Skills

My main skills are persistence and knowing my limitations. I mostly do not give up and know there is nearly always a technical solution to most problems. My worst skill is presenting stuff to people. It took me 20 years to realise that, but it's a relief now that I know. It also took me 40 years to realise I have a bad sense of direction. That's probably a man thing, to do with overconfidence. I'm impatient, intolerant, and often grumpy. On the surface, not great qualities for community building, but maybe good qualities for getting things done. I like working with people who are honest, intelligent, fast, know stuff, know their limits and laugh.

I love and hate community. I love and hate meetings. I love and hate running. I'm generally ambivalent to everything. I have an ideal image of what community will look like and how people will relate. When that does happen occasionally, say in a meeting, even with only 70% of boxes ticked, I love it, though it very rarely happens.

Risk Taking

Risk taking is necessary to start a cohousing community. This is probably the single most important

way I have succeeded. My philosophy about risk taking is that it doesn't really exist. I don't include gambling and mad stuff. I mean risks with a realistic payback. Risk taking is a balance of risks. Doing something scary might actually be a lower risk than not doing it. Taken to an extreme, the zero risk state might mean you don't go outside but hide under your duvet, thinking it's safe. That apparent safe state could lead to depression, loneliness, lack of fitness and low self esteem. If you don't take the apparent big risk, you may never achieve what you want and may regret it.

Risking all your money and more i.e. borrowing from banks, does often yield amazing results, though it's crucial to have an escape plan if the project fails. In the case of buying land or a property, that escape plan may mean selling it fast at auction or to an under bidder. It's wise to calculate what the maximum loss is likely to be and ask yourself how that would feel. It may be every penny you have. Of course that low feeling has to be balanced against the ecstatic feeling of beginning the journey of creating a new community or other venture.

Risk taking and how I feel about it, is hugely important for everything I do. Sometimes I need to force myself to do the calculation of balancing the risks. The risks

may be emotional, loss of friendship, health as well as money. So when people say I am risk averse or low risk, that's not true. Every intelligent person is risk averse. What they really mean is that they let the fear win and opt for an apparently safe option.

Having given all this excellent advice, I am invariably terrified and shaking with fear hours after exchanging contracts on a big project, especially when I've risked more money than I have. A week after Helen and I bought the land for Springhill Cohousing in 2000, I asked the receivers whether I could break the contract and lose the deposit money of £150,000, they refused and held me to the seven months completion. Fear is very strong. Another potential cohousing project in Bristol resulted in me losing £40,000. I got scared about contaminated land, and I caught flu, which made me even more scared. I asked the seller for the under-bidder's details and sold the land at a loss, two days after exchanging contracts. I was initially relieved and then regretted it. I was not following my own advice.

The last thing about risk taking that I would like to share is to not do a lot of reading and research, apart from reading this short guide! Burying your head in the sand can have benefits, it's not as bad as people claim. The principle is, the more you read, the more you learn about the risks including imaginary and low probability risks. That might scare the pants off you, so you don't proceed. That happened to me twice with contaminated land. Both projects turned out to have not been as risky as I thought and would have been manageable.

Many large infrastructure projects like the Channel Tunnel would not have even started if they had been researched properly. The tunnel cost double the calculated cost. That initial build figure was not a guess, it cost thousands of pounds for professionals to calculate how much it would cost, building in risk factors and adding in a margin. They got it massively wrong. But because they got it wrong, it was possible to get the finance and start building. Then when costs doubled they had to find the extra money because they were committed and didn't want to lose everything they'd spent.

Finance

One of the easiest ways of getting finance to purchase a property is to borrow from the seller. You will have to make this very attractive to the seller, especially as they may not be keen on having an ongoing involvement in the property they have sold.

The benefit to you, the buyer, is that you don't have to convince the bank of the value of the property, especially if it's unusual. There is no need for a credit check on you or your community organisation. If it's a large amount you are borrowing and you have no track record in property development, a regular bank is unlikely to consider you lending-worthy and you may fail a credit check. There are specialist banks who will provide bridging finance, with no status checks and often no formal valuation. They charge much higher interest rates and usually only for a period of up to 12 months.

The seller, however, will certainly agree that the value is the price you have agreed. If your offer is considerably more than others, they may accept the annoyance of lending you money for, say, 12 months. I have done this with three out of four cohousing properties. When I bought the land from the receiver for Springhill Cohousing, I offered £550,000. I had £150,000 savings which I used as the deposit. I asked for a delayed completion of 12 months and to pay 5% interest on the remaining £400,000. Paying a relatively high interest rate makes the offer more attractive.

That meant I had 12 months to find enough members to join and pay back the balance. We managed to complete in only four months and pay all the money back, plus interest. Members joined very quickly and eagerly. The attraction was that when we had the land, it was real. The architects had drawn the layout design, so members could see what they were buying into. It was an attractive and realistic package. The architects at this stage were working at risk, and were not paid. They were very excited by designing the first cohousing project in

the UK. The downside to members joining was that they had to agree to pay whatever it would cost to build, they were given a rough estimate, which was exceeded. Most members disliked not knowing the final cost of their house. They eventually paid only 50% of the market value.

Delayed completion is one method of borrowing from the seller. Another is to give them a first legal charge on the property. For example, with Springhill Cohousing, the land went for closed tenders. I only heard from the bank on a Friday and offers with cash deposits had to be submitted on the following Monday. They would then exchange contracts unilaterally with whichever party they chose. This is fairly normal practice with large housing developers. I knew I had to outbid them and to pay even more to compensate for not paying the full amount within 28 days. The bank re-possessed the land the week before from the firm of accountants with whom I had been negotiating. They didn't tell me, I only found out by asking a lot of people.

Borrowing money from future residents is an excellent method. That may mean selling theit houses and renting. Having ready cash means any group is in a very good position. Sometimes you have to move fast to get the property. At auction, when your bid is accepted you have to pay a 10% deposit immediately and the balance in 28 days, sometimes less.

Banks are there to lend money. They can be very helpful. You need a good business plan and a cashflow forecast. Selling the vision to the bank is essential. Explaining how they would get their money back if disaster struck is what the bank needs to know. The larger the deposit you have the easier it is, as that means their risk is lower. They probably would only consider lending with at least a 30% deposit. Approaching the bank or building society you use for personal finance is worth trying, especially if you have a relationship with the manager. Unfortunately, most bank lending is now done centrally and managers may not even be able to make decisions.

When I bought Frankleigh House in Wiltshire at auction, I won the bid at £285,000. That meant paying a 10% deposit of £28,500. The five families each contracted £5,000, so that almost paid for it. We then had 28 days to pay the balance of £256,000. Triodos bank was new in the UK in 1995. A manager visited the property the next day and offered a full mortgage within 10 days. My subsequent experience with Triodos has been awful. For instance for Springhill, they wanted various reports costing £10,000. Over 4 months, they strung us along with promises but no firm offer and we lost the £10,000. I approached the Co-op Bank after four months of teasing from Triodos. The Co-op agreed to lend development finance of £3.5 million within two weeks. I would not, however, recommend bidding at auction if you don't have the whole of the purchase price. I did have emergency bridging finance in place, in case Triodos didn't lend.

Buying Land and/or Buildings

This is the hardest step and the most important by far, in my opinion. Many, many aspiring cohousing groups get together, meet for years, have picnics, go on camping trips, form limited companies and write vision statements. If they don't buy or acquire a property for the community, it won't happen and they have failed in their aspirations. Although they may have successfully made a lovely community of friends.

Finding a property or site is not difficult, it depends how fussy you are and how much money you have or can raise. This may be obvious, but it's worth saying. The more constraints you have, for example: the location has to be in Norwich, has to be at least five acres, has to be an old mansion or has to be new build... the lower your probability of successfully buying a property. Try suspending all constraints, and just search for development land, large buildings, farms, caravan  sites and industrial sites. You may be pleasantly surprised to discover a place you would never have normally considered.

The obvious channels for searching are local and national estate agents, land agents, and auctioneers. It's worth subscribing to *Estates Gazette* (the developers' bible, as it has many adverts for land). Contact utility companies, search the Land Registry online (make sure not to choose one of the many bogus cloned websites). The Land Registry online allows you to find out who owns bits of land. It costs £3 per search and another £3 for the title plan. Let all your friends know you are looking. Let people know on social media.

If the property is within the town or city settlement boundary, then development is presumed possible. Buying a field somewhere in the countryside means it's almost impossible to get permission. Get good planning advice by reading. Now is the time to disregard what I said above about not reading. Become an expert. You can arrange a pre-planning meeting with the local authority, many of them now charge a small amount. I try not to spend any money at all before land purchase, apart from maybe £100 or so. This would be on things like building a website and booking the occasional meeting room. Many people will disagree with this and say you should spend a lot on surveys and assessments. If you buy somewhere with residential planning permission that makes things much easier and lowers the risk. It won't have permission for a cohousing community but the question of whether you can have a residential development has been established.

Read the section on taking risks, above. Buying without planning permission or with any problems e.g. contaminated land, means the land will be cheaper. That cheaper price might be the difference between making the project happen or not. It is a big risk buying without any permission but can be worthwhile. Your escape plan is to sell the land. Hopefully you'll get around what you paid for it, but allow for a shortfall: that calculated loss is your risk money.

A very big mistake people make when buying property is to try to get a bargain. They may bid low in tender competition or at auction. I don't think there are any bargains or below market value properties. That would only be the case if you managed to deceive someone or the seller was not well informed about the market. I generally bid quite high, so that I win at auction at the tender stage. My thinking is that the other bidders or potential buyers are only wanting to buy in order to make a profit, whereas we want to build a cohousing community, and that is worth a lot more than the (arguably) extra amount you might have paid. Cohousing buyers always have an advantage over commercial buyers. That sounds counter-intuitive because we are brought up to think large companies have more power than us.

Design

Before Springhill Cohousing started, I'd had several meetings with architects Pat Borer of the Centre for Alternative Technology and Jono Hines of Archetype. They were both very keen and happy to work at risk until we bought the land. Jono produced a draft layout of the site and house designs. These were really important for people to see clearly what they were buying into, even though for most people they bought in re-planning permission, meaning that these initial drawings were just intentions. The initial layout can be seen on the archived website cohouses.net.

After we bought land, Jono Hines attended most meetings. He took his design brief from the meeting and produced revisions for the next meeting. In hindsight this was a difficult process. Especially during the planning application stage. For example, after our first application was refused because the timber cladding was out of keeping with the surroundings, I would normally immediately re-apply addressing the objections and re-submit using bricks, with a view to later re-applying for the material we wanted after we had secured permission. A few members objected strongly to this strategy, saying it was dishonest. I was shocked and terrified that I had created an irrational monster that would destroy the project. These people would make wonderful community members but they knew nothing about property development and did not want to take advice. This illustrated the single biggest problem: I had invited members to become equal directors of the development company. I thought that was idealistic and right, however, it was not honest, as I did not want their input into matters outside their expertise. In subsequent projects, members were asked to make well defined and limited design choices. That worked well and was not overwhelming. I offered fixed prices, meaning members had cost certainty. That meant I took the risk of cost increases. The designs were all inspired

by Danish cohousing models and the book *The Pattern Language* by Christopher Alexander.

Recruiting Members and Joining

My first cohousing project, Frankleigh Cohousing, was made of five families from London, three of which homeschooled their children. We lived in London and all knew each other. For the second project, Springhill, 80% of people came via the website, now archived – www.cohouses.net. That was in 2000, so the internet was fairly new. In those days people would ask for stuff to be posted to them. I explained that was not possible and they had to go to the library, if necessary to access the website. Other methods were articles in national papers including *The Guardian*, *Financial Times*, *The Independent* and *The Observer*. Two members joined after reading about the project in *Positive News*[1]. Flyers on café noticeboards were useful, and of course members recruited their friends.

New members met me upstairs in Woodruffs Café in Stroud town centre. People were very keen and understood the concept. I made a point of not persuading anyone. In fact the opposite, I wanted people to be very keen. Any doubts expressed were amplified by me, I explained the financial risks of not knowing the end price and all the other unknowns. I tried to dissuade many people. This unintentional negative selling often made people more keen. On the first meeting, unknown

1   The old articles are available via this link: www.springhill.co/articles.html

people would eagerly hand me a cheque for £35,000. I clearly came across as very trustworthy and missed out on a career as a con-artist.

After joining, which meant paying for their plot and signing the agreement, the new members were invited to the next monthly meeting. Naturally prospective members asked whether they could meet existing members first, to inform their decision whether to join. I explained that was not possible. There was no selection process other than agreeing to the principles of cohousing and being able to buy in. Nearly all members had joined without meeting others first. Before I started the project, I believed that it was essential to vet new members, otherwise we might get really unsuitable people. However, I had read accounts from some residents in US cohousing communities about how bad selection processes can be, both in the workplace and elsewhere. According to them, selection would lend itself to unconscious racism, as we tend to choose people who seem similar to ourselves. Plus, they said that, in general, selection processes and recruitment practices do not work well. This convinced me, and now there is still no vetting in any of the projects.

Constitution and Legals

I spent virtually no money before we bought the land on each project. I wrote the documents needed for members to join, the loan agreements, and the commitment to pay whatever the build cost would be. All written in simple English without a lawyer. I bought the limited company for £25 and issued paper share certificates. Our lawyers, Comptons, drafted the Lease. I gave them a sheet of A4 with all our requirements. The lease requirements were that members had to agree to the principles as set in the cohousing book (giving an example of being on the cooking rota), and that they had to join the Residents Association and abide by its agreements. The Lease is our constitution. Each house has a 999 year lease. We have three levels of hierarchy: the shareholders at the top, the directors (each shareholder can appoint two directors), and lastly, the Residents Association. The latter, in practice, makes 99% of the decisions and includes all residents, including tenants and lodgers.

One exciting element to include in the Lease is a clause that donates 1% (or more) of any future sales to the Residents' Association. It provides a valuable and painless source of income. Estate Agents' fees can be over 2%, and as – usually – future members are found via networking, no agents' fees are payable.

Ownership/Tenure

In Denmark they have a huge number of cohousing communities with every sort of tenure, from 100% social housing to mixed rentals to private ownership and hybrid models. The four projects I founded were all private ownership. That means that individuals can rent out their houses and have lodgers. All residents have to agree to the principles and to be a member of the Residents Association. The tenancy agreements and lodgers agreements must each have an appropriate cohousing clause. We have samples for members to use.

Building Works and Contracts

I prefer a building contract known as Design and Build. Initially this is probably the most expensive contract because the builder takes on all the risks involved in foundations and other unknowns. The advantage

is that you know the end cost at the beginning and you as a client can have as much input as you like with detailed design. If, say, you choose a fancier door than the contractor has chosen, you pay the difference, and the same if it's cheaper.

I used Design and Build for Lansdown Cohousing[2] and it worked very well. Springhill ended up with Design and Build, but started off with a Project

2 Lansdown and Sladbrook Cohousing website: www.coflats.com

Management Contract. That was another regret, as the members group chose that because they thought we'd get more design control. It meant ever escalating prices and less control.

Archetype supervised the project. My job at Springhill during development was to liaise with all the parties including the bank, who paid monthly in arrears. I was not impressed with the Quantity Surveyor who charged 0.75% of the total build cost and in return

gave wildly low predicted build costs. They have a conflict of interest, they get paid more if costs go up! I have never used a QS since. I believe in the US, they are not used and they laugh at us paying someone who has no liability for their valuations.

Decision Making and Group Process

Forming a group that will eventually live together in your exciting new cohousing community can start a long time before move-in day. That means the community of people will know each other pretty well. They will have already cooked together, argued with each other, been on trips to the beach and had long, difficult and sometimes fun meetings.

The process of designing the community can be a cohesive and community building exercise. In order for that process to happen well, the decision making process and how to manage meetings needs to be agreed. There are many well thought out systems. Training can be very useful. Choosing good effective trainers experienced with consensus decision making can be very difficult, as there are few experts who offer themselves as trainers.

Before the cohousing group is formed and opened up, there may be just you or a small core group. This is the ideal time to make immutable principles. For instance, all the food in the common house must be plant-based, or no dogs in the community, or all electricity must be generated on site. It is possible that discussions on any

of the four Ps (parenting, parking, pets and paint colours) can cause the group irretrievable damage and split. So it's important to get anything that's crucial to you in the original documents to which members need to agree.

To make the principles unchangeable, they need to be written into the lease or governing instrument. In the early stages a simple document that you draw up can say that these principles will eventually be in the lease. There needs to be a lock to prevent making future changes. This is done by saying any modification to the principle needs a unanimous decision of all members, or 75%... or whatever else you want. Obviously only include immutable principles if they would prevent you or someone in the core group from joining the community. These are not preferences, those can be agreed upon with the larger group by consensus. These immutable principles can make the community feel safe and more appealing to some prospective members and repel others who may find them controlling and undemocratic. The other important thing to define is how members can leave the group.

Decision making during the development phase and the building of the physical community is very different from making decisions when everyone lives together in the cohousing community. This entails having a hierarchy, which will not exist after move-in. The core group or managing director needs to have executive powers to make many of the day-to-day business decisions.

It's far smoother to spell out exactly what decisions the larger group can make e.g. design of the common house, design of individual house interiors, the gardens, meal frequency and how cooking will work, the laundry etc. Be aware of the four Ps[3]. Explain what the role of the core group or managing director is,

3   These four Ps are very common points of heated debate in cohousing.

and how much they are paid, if appropriate. Say if they can be fired by the larger group and if so how, or if not, then when does their job ends. Make the boundaries between the core group and larger group crystal clear.

The system we aspire to use at Springhill Cohousing[4] involves using three coloured cards: red, green and orange. During the discussion phase the cards are used instead of putting up your hand. There is a descending hierarchy of red, green and orange that the chairperson should follow. A red card means a process intervention e.g. "Someone is crying and I'd like to have a five minute pause", or "This is completely off topic and we have limited time and a full agenda". A green card means "I have some relevant information e.g. "The outside lights have already been fixed, we don't need to discuss them". An orange card is like putting your hand up to express yourself. It is chosen after the red and green cards, even if the person was first to show their orange card.

The decision phase is where the group sees if there is consent for a proposal. The proposal may have been modified during discussion. At any time, someone can ask for a show of cards. This illustrates where people are with the proposal. It can be at the beginning of the discussion, in the middle and at the end. A green card means that you are for the proposal with slight reservations. An orange card means you have serious reservations and are not ready to give consent. A red card means you think the proposal is fundamentally against the agreed principles and that you will want to block consent.

The meeting ingredients I personally need are:

a) very short and clearly spoken inputs

b) not spilling over e.g. not showing how clever you are, unless you are explicit about that and it's appropriate

c) having a consensus about consensus procedures and adhering to it

d) allowable interruptions using card system

e) respecting others doesn't mean allowing
    people to talk for a long time or going
    off topic. It does mean listening without
    immediately constructing a reply

f) respecting and liking everyone in
    the room and believing they will use
    the agreed consensus system

g) concise inclusive agendas with relevant
    information pre-submitted, not being given
    loads of paper or a slide show in the meeting.

These ingredients are similar to what I want when
living in community. I also need members to have
done some personal therapy or introspection, so that
they are able to ask themselves why they behave as
they do, to have a sense of humour and to try not to
presume but ask. I am definitely guilty of presuming
and sometimes not knowing what my real motives are.

One important thing for me, and possibly one of the
hardest things for me to do, is to un-own a proposal.
This means putting the proposal on the table and step-
ping back to join the group. You may have spent ages
formulating it, on your own or with others. That means
it's likely you have a lot invested in the proposal. That's
why it might be very hard to let go. The advantages of
letting go are that the proposal is no longer a personal,
ego-invested item. Secondly, letting go enables you to be
critical of it and be open to suggestions. It allows or frees

others to support it, who
may naturally have taken
the role of questioning and
being critical. If all goes
well the proposal should
develop and improve. The
modifications will mean
that it has a wider group
ownership and does not
have a person or persons
associated with it. This is
not easy, but an aspiration.

Be aware of unconscious
personal agendas and
inappropriate agenda
items. An unconscious
personal agenda is some-

A note on how to make consensus proposals

1) Try to make the proposal open and describing an intention, rather than something very specific. This allows the meeting to know what's behind it and build the detailed proposal by consensus, eg. "To make the middle floor more beautiful" instead of "paint the south wall pink".

2) An open proposal is less likely to be confrontational as it's hard to disagree with making something more beautiful but you may hate pink.

3) Respond to a proposal by seeking more information, so that you know more about what the issues are. Try not to oppose a proposal as your first response. That can come across as you are not listening and being reactive, eg "I'd like to remove the tree blocking my light" If you respond with "I really love that tree" then a confrontation has began. Instead, you can ask more about the light, how they feel about the tree and ask what other options there may be.

4) Sometimes a specific proposal is needed. It's best to research the costs and logistics. Asking members for the options allows them to feel ownership and that they are part of the decision.

5) Inviting people to join a group in order to formulate a proposal can be useful and supportive and encourages members to own the decision making process.

---

thing that we carry with us and want to be satisfied. This may run counter to an efficient and fun meeting. Examples are: "I am lonely and want company", "I want to be appreciated", or "I want to show how much I know". These unconscious agendas will inevitably slip into the meeting. Group training can help address them. So can organising other events and informal meetings. Showing off and wanting to be appreciated are both fine and human desires. But it's important that you ask for those things openly and with the knowledge of others e.g. stand up comedy.

Announcements or discussions about where, say, a picnic should be (and can be) done efficiently via email or at a non-business meeting. Or you can just arrange it and announce the time and see who turns up.

For a good decision, proposals should be discussed well beforehand in pre-meetings and via email. That allows members time to consider the proposals and ask questions and chat informally. The agenda should be published at least three days ahead of the meeting. Try not to have Any Other Business items, they are items for another meeting and no one will have had notice of them. If you can't make the meeting there is no need to announce that, unless you want to change the meeting time. If an initial show of cards has a few orange and red cards, then it makes sense to withdraw the proposal. Work on it more, get feedback, have more pre-meetings. People may just not be ready for your idea, so park it for a few months.

Minutes should record only decisions. The minute taker should as far as possible read out what they propose to minute before the chairperson asks for consent. This is so that the proposal is very clear and prevents people later saying "that's not what I thought we agreed". The minute taker should not add further notes later. Of course, anyone can write an informal report giving a flavour of the meeting.

Conclusion

Cohousing is an amazing way to live. It's really simple to build a cohousing community. The way to succeed is to remove as many obstacles as possible. This includes not looking for the ideal site, compromising a lot, but not on core values. You will make loads of mistakes, that's fine, many of them can be addressed later. Secondly, be aware of the risk you take in not doing it. Regrets are rubbish and life is short.

We use words like eco-housing and sustainability. Remember that what is best ecological practice today, will probably be poor practice in 20 years. But in my view, cohousing as a way for humans to live together, will still be state of the art for many years to come.

David Michael
has founded four cohousing communities. He studied maths and psychology at university. He was active in anti-patriarchal men's groups. He worked as a school teacher, under five's worker, a psychotherapist and a builder. He stood for both UK and EU Parliaments (for the Free Transport Party: www.freetransport.org) and home schooled two daughters and has been a vegan since 2017.

What is this Coliving Thing, Anyway?

PENNY CLARK

Communal living goes commercial. If you don't want to clean the communal sink then why not consider coliving?

Coliving or co-living has become a catch-all term for living together, but confusingly, it is also the name used to describe a relatively new iteration of urban communal living – the professionally managed kind. Rather than this type of coliving conjuring images of assorted mugs in the kitchen cupboard, chore rotas on chalk boards and jumbled wellies in the porch, it evokes chic lobbies, long, hotel-like corridors, and events programmes. So, what is this coliving thing, anyway? This article looks at what it is, different types of coliving, the origins and growth of coliving, why it is rising in popularity, and what we might make of this commercialised version of communal living.

Defining coliving

Coliving can be defined as managed (usually rented) accommodation, where residents have their own private space but share communal areas, and where there is an emphasis on community. Most coliving spaces will have one or more staff with the job title like 'Host' or 'Community Manager', who have a responsibility to look after residents and facilitate social connection. Convenience is also highly important in coliving, with residents able to sign up for short-term, 'hassle-free' contracts with one fee encompassing rent and utilities, as well as opting in for extra services such as room cleaning.

How coliving spaces are designed and operated differs, though there are a few loose categories which most fit into, which I describe below.

Networked homes

Networked homes are in essence a group of HMOs (houses of multiple occupation) or flatshares which are scattered across a city, country, or countries. Usually, coliving operators will enable and encourage their residents to move easily between these properties if they would like to, and will also link these properties together through a strong brand identity and the occasional event (e.g. Friday drinks, pot lucks). In these properties, residents will have a private bedroom, will sometimes have a private bathroom, but otherwise share all other spaces. In calling what is essentially a house or flat share 'coliving', operators are expected to provide a certain level of convenience and service, for example having one fee for everything (rent, bills, etc.), high-spec design, good wi-fi, high quality communal areas, and in some cases, enabling current residents to have a say in who moves in next.

Example: Pollen Co-living

Pollen Co-Living has several HMO-style properties in South London, with bills-included rents ranging from £650-£950 per month, and a 6 month minimum tenancy. Homes are aimed at young professionals, with the promise of taking care of the admin so that residents can "get on with living".

Mid-scale coliving

Mid-scale coliving consists of buildings which house circa 20-80 residents, usually for between 3-18 months. Residents will have either studios or shared flats, as well as access to shared amenities, which may include living areas, coworking, laundry, kitchens and outdoor space. There will be a roster of events, both put on by the coliving company and by residents (e.g. yoga classes, tapas nights, talks), and services such as room cleaning and a concierge will be available.

Example: Mason & Fifth

Mason & Fifth is a wellness-focussed coliving operator. They operate a building in Bermondsey, London, containing 28 studios and a 92 square metre communal area, consisting mainly of a lounge area, kitchen and coworking space, plus an outdoor patio area. They place a strong emphasis on facilitating social interaction and wellbeing amongst residents. Events include fitness classes, meditation, breathwork and talking circles. Rents, which include bills, events and additional resources, start at £2000 per month, with 3 month+ tenancies.

Large-scale, purpose-built coliving

This category of coliving includes buildings which house anything from 80 to 500+ residents, and is often purpose-built. As with networked homes and mid-scale coliving, stays are usually from 3 to 18 months. Residents' private space will typically consist of a studio apartment, and they will have access to extensive shared amenity space. Amenities often include: laundry facilities, shared kitchens, social spaces, and a front desk. There may also be amenities such as a gym, co-working space, games room, outdoor/exercise area, cinema room, bar, restaurant, or on-site shop. There will be an extensive roster of events, and services which will include cleaning and a concierge.

Example: Folk

Folk Co-living has two buildings in operation: one in Harrow, North London, with 220 studios, and one in Earlsfield, South London, with 315 studios. Both buildings have extensive shared spaces and amenities. For example, the Harrow site includes a gym, TV room, restaurant and bar, laundry and pool table, reading room, large communal kitchen, terrace area, outdoor gym space, cycle storage, coworking and parking spaces. Events include rooftop pilates, litter-picking, Friday drinks, and classes e.g. 'Blockchain 101'. Rents include everything but TV licences and room cleaning, and range from £1425 to £2070 per month, with 3 month+ tenancies.

Coliving for remote workers

This type of coliving is aimed at location-independent workers (the so-called 'digital nomad'), who may spend some or all of their time moving between different countries. Coliving buildings for remote workers typically house between 20-35 residents. Residents may have their own rooms, or may share with others, hostel-style. Indeed, this type of coliving evolved from and intersects with the hostel model, though is catered more towards residents staying for a longer period of time (weeks or months). There is an emphasis on residents getting to know one another, spending time together, and engaging with the local community. This is facilitated by operators through events (organised by the operator and suggested by residents) and local partnerships.

Coconat is a rural 'workation' retreat, based in a small village outside of Berlin. There is a range of accommodation options including dormitories, glamping and camping. The space is advertised for both individual and group bookings, with the option to stay for as little as one night. Amenities include a variety of coworking spaces, fast wi-fi, an onsite restaurant and shop, and sauna. Additional services include massage and yoga. The operators also run events which involve the local community, such as their yearly 'Applefest'.

Pod coliving

Pod coliving takes the concept of minimising private space and maximising shared space to a greater extreme. Coliving residents have their own bed space in a shared dorm (sometimes an enclosed 'pod' space), and otherwise share spaces with other residents. This model emphasises affordability, and may also be more transient than coliving communities with greater levels of private space.

Haven is a coliving company based in Los Angeles, which is focussed on wellness and personal growth, and is primarily aimed at young professionals. Rents begin at $995 per month. Residents have shared dorms, along with communal spaces including coworking spaces, gym/yoga studios, and outdoor spaces, along with weekly events, communal dinners, cleaning, wifi and utilities.

Hybrid models

It is increasingly common for coliving to be part of a hybrid model of accommodation. For example, a company may combine a hotel model with a coliving model; or a hostel may convert to coliving during the off season. Hybridisation goes beyond just accommodation, with some companies offering a 'live-work-play' dynamic, in which residents are able to access coworking memberships along with a social calendar, plus on-site restaurants/bars etc. The intermingling of accommodation types and other revenue sources can increase potential revenue streams and the resilience of the business model.

Example: The Social Hub

Student accommodation, hotel, coworking, coliving hybrid, with locations in 14 different European cities. Offers high-spec, playful design, with on-site food & beverage offerings, events calendar, and premium price-tag. As there is a combination of hotel guests, long-stay guests and students, residents can stay from anything from one night to one year.

The origins and growth of coliving

It isn't known where the term 'coliving' first came from, though it is widely accepted as being intertwined with the concept of coworking. A number of journalists and online writers attribute the emergence of the term to so-called 'hacker houses' in San Francisco.[1]

1   Wood, H. (2017) 'Co-living 2030: Are you ready for the Sharing Economy?', Archinect Features; Xie, J. (2013) 'One Answer to San Francisco's Overpriced Housing: "Co-Living"', CityLab, 2 December.

Hacker houses, which are mainly a US phenomenon, are house-shares in which fledging tech entrepreneurs live in close quarters to save on rent costs, whilst attempting to get their start-up enterprise off the ground. Seen as a cheap rental option in otherwise prohibitively expensive cities such as New York and San Francisco, life in a hacker house comes with the expectation that living conditions will be basic, and that cleanliness, health and safety and personal space will be at a minimum! (For a vivid description involving cockroaches and missing shower heads, see Andrew Frawley's 2017 article.[2]) There is also an expectation that residents will support and stimulate one another as entrepreneurs. It is believed that coliving emerged from the hacker house concept, to solve the problem of prospective renters who were moving to expensive cities where they knew few people. So, while coliving has always been commercial, its origins appear to be grounded in a rough and ready form of intentional community that in itself is centered around commercial endeavour, in creating a mutually supportive environment for professional growth.

As the sector matures, those in 'sister' real estate niches such as PBSA (purpose-built student accommodation), build-to-rent, and multifamily[3] have influenced and been influenced by the coliving model, and we now see more large-scale, purpose-built shared living on the horizon.

Coliving is on the rise in the UK, as well as in Europe,[4] the US,[5] and Asia (in particular China[6] and India[7]). A 2022 report by Savills found that there are 24,000 total pipeline and operational coliving units in the UK, with demand being highest in

2 Frawley, A. (2017) 'Bunk beds, roaches and nerdy geniuses: my year in a Silicon Valley hacker house', The Guardian, 8 September. Available at: www.theguardian.com/usnews/2017/sep/08/tech-silicon-valley-san-francisco-entrepreneur (Accessed: 10 February 2023).

3 A residential building with more than one housing unit, e.g. a block of flats.

4 JLL (2019) 'European Coliving Index'. Available at: residential.jll.co.uk/insights/research/jll-european-coliving-index-2019 (Accessed: 4 March 2023).

5 Cushman & Wakefield (2020) 'Coliving during COVID-19'. Available at: www.cushmanwakefield.com/en/insights/covid-19/coliving-during-covid-19 (Accessed 4 March 2023).

6 Kumar, A. and Hatti, C. (2019) 'Global Coliving Report, 2019'. Available at: thehousemonk.com/reports/ (Accessed: 4 March 2023).

7 JLL (2019) 'Co-Living Reshaping Rental Housing in India'. Available at: www.jll.co.in/en/trends-and-insights/research/co-living-reshaping-rental-housing-in-india (Accessed: 4 March 2023).

London, as well as other large UK cities, such as Manchester, Leeds, Birmingham, and Edinburgh.[8] Given this momentum, the question is not whether coliving is here to stay, but rather what direction it will take as the sector grows.

Why is coliving rising in popularity?

Coliving is in part a response to a lack of affordable and high quality rental housing in cities. When comparing 2017 with 2007, the number of UK rented households has risen by 63%.[9] Arguably, this is due to a combination of home ownership becoming financially out of reach for many,[10] along with higher levels of geographical transience, and people marrying and having children later in life.[11] [12] This has led to a greater demand for rental housing, and a relatively wealthier group of people who are renting, when compared with the recent past. As such, the private rental sector has become increasingly professionalised, as investors, developers and operators have recognised the gap in the market.

Coliving is especially appealing to those who are moving to a new city, perhaps to start a new job, or to study. It offers them a safe 'landing pad', where residents can have 'hassle-free' living, flexible lease terms, and a social network, all in one place. Indeed, coliving residents are most often young local and international professionals and students.[13] However, this is not the whole story. Coliving homes are popu-

8   Savills (2022) 'Spotlight: UK Co-living – a market poised for huge growth. Available at: www.savills.co.uk/research_articles/229130/328949-0 (Accessed: 4 March 2023).

9   ONS (2019) 'UK private rented sector: 2018'. Available at: www.ons.gov.uk/economy/inflationandpriceindices/articles/ukprivaterentedsector/2018 (Accessed: 4 March 2023).

10   Partington, R. (2019) 'Home ownership amongst young adults has "collapsed", study finds', The Guardian, 16 February. Available at: www.theguardian.com/money/2018/feb/16/homeownership-among-young-adults-collapsed-institute-fiscal-studies (Accessed: 4 March 2023).

11   ONS (2019) 'Marriages in England and Wales: 2016'. Available at: www.ons.gov.uk/peoplepopulationandcommunity/birthsdeathsandmarriages/marriagecohabitationandcivilpartnerships/bulletins/marriagesinenglandandwalesprovisional/2016 (Accessed: 4 March 2023).

12   ONS (2019) 'Birth characteristics in England and Wales'. Available at: www.ons.gov.uk/peoplepopulationandcommunity/birthsdeathsandmarriages/livebirths/bulletins/birthcharacteristicsinenglandandwales/2017 (Accessed: 4 March 2023).

13   ULI (2022) 'The ULI and JLL European Coliving Best Practice Guide'. Available at: www.jll.co.uk/en/trends-and-insights/research/the-european-coliving-best-practice-guide (Accessed: 4 March 2023).

lated by a mix of people, from couples, those in their forties and fifties, to those who are retired. Coliving tends to attract people who are in moments of life transition, whether that's moving to a different city or country to start a new job, breaking up with a partner, or considering what to do now that the kids have left home.

In such moments of life transition, the appeal of a readymade social network may be strong. Over the past few years, some of the pernicious impacts of loneliness have been revealed. We now know that loneliness is worse for your health than smoking 15 cigarettes per day, and can increase your risk of coronary heart disease and stroke.[14] Whilst this issue has pierced civic consciousness (e.g. the appointment of a Minister for Loneliness in 2018), as ever, the wheels of real estate are slow to turn. Coliving is one of the few responses from the housing sector which actively foregrounds our needs for social connection.

The willingness of residents to adopt coliving may also have some basis in there being a highly similar, well-known model of housing: student halls. With around half of young people now attending university[15] – many of whom will experience living in student accommodation – coliving is less likely to be considered 'weird', and may even feel like a natural next step for graduates. This, along with the normalisation of sharing cars (Zipcar, Uber, Blablacar), everyday objects (Library of Things, Freecycle, Gumtree) and homes (Couchsurfing, Airbnb, Spareroom), may mean that coliving feels in-step with the so-called 'sharing economy'.

Finally, its rapid rise must also be attributed to the perceived effectiveness of the business model, and a large potential market. For the foreseeable future, it is likely that housing in cities will be scarce and expensive, and that the number of people renting their homes will continue to grow. As high-density urban housing, there is a strong financial case to invest in coliving, and as its track record of success grows, so does investor lending.[16]

4   Campaign to end loneliness (no date) 'Facts about loneliness'. Available at: www.campaigntoendloneliness.org/facts-and-statistics/ (Accessed: 4 March 2023).

5   GOV.UK (2019) 'Participation Rates in Higher Education: 2006 to 2018'. Available at: www.gov.uk/government/statistics/participation-rates-in-higher-education-2006-to-2018 (Accessed: 4 March 2023).

6   Savills (2022) 'Spotlight: UK Co-living – a market poised for huge growth. Available at: www.savills.co.uk/research_articles/229130/328949-0 (Accessed: 4 March 2023).

What to make of it all?

Coliving is a controversial form of housing, which has both been posited as offering "very real solutions to many of the problems we face today",[17] and as a "cynical ploy by property developers to cash in on a generation living in the 'age of loneliness'".[18] To begin with, and as is true for all communal living typologies, it is reductive to treat coliving as a homogenous group. There are different models, buildings, operators, staff and residents, all with unique contexts that shift over time. Nevertheless, in this section I explore how we might think about this recent iteration of communal living.

One highly contested point of discussion is affordability. The popularity of coliving has, in-part, been related to its affordability by numerous real estate advisory firms,[19] yet a glance at most prices being charged by UK operators may have you thinking otherwise. A recent report which surveyed coliving residents across five different countries found that residents earned, on average, 1.6x more than the gross national income.[20] Whilst there are definitions of 'Affordable Housing' with a capital 'A', affordability as a concept is relative, and research which argues for the relative affordability of coliving is usually comparing it with renting a one-bed flat or studio in the same city, plus the price of bills and a gym membership (costs which are usually included in coliving).[21] Indeed, the economies of scale involved in coliving enable a more cost-effective lifestyle for those who would otherwise be renting alone in a one bed or studio, plus offers access to luxuries – such as rooftop swimming pools, cookery classes and concierge services – that otherwise are financially out of reach for most. Beyond the roof over people's heads, the thing that arguably offers residents the greatest benefit – community – is the most nebulous and most difficult to value by any traditional means in real estate. It is also something which should not only be available to the more well

---

17 Cleaver, N. and Frearson, A. (2021). All Together Now: The co-living and co-working revolution. London: RIBA Publishing.

18 Coldwell, W. (2019) '"Co-living": the end of urban loneliness – or cynical corporate dormitories?'. Available at: www.theguardian.com/cities/2019/sep/03/co-living-the-end-of-urban-loneliness-or-cynicalcorporate-dormitories (Accessed: 1 March 2023).

19 See, for example: Cushman & Wakefield (2019) 'Survey of the Co-Living Landscape'; CBRE (2020) 'Europe Co-living Report'; ULI (2022) 'ULI and JLL European Coliving Best Practice Guide'.

20 Worldwide Coliving Membership (2023) 'Flexible Living Trend Report 2023 Vol. 1'. Available at: www.epsd.co.kr/en/wcm/ (Accessed: 5 March 2023).

21 See the latter two reports mentioned in footnote 19.

off. As Diana Lind writes in her book, Brave New Home, "To get co-living to work for average renters, the current branding needs to shift toward efficiency rather than convenience"[22] and the high-end amenities and services that entails. There is certainly potential for more affordable versions of coliving: perhaps they could look like something closer to house-sharing intentional communities. However, it appears that the industry is currently moving in the opposite direction, with continued investment and focus on large-scale coliving, which offers the highest yields.[23]

Coliving promises 'community',[24] and in fact packages community as part of the service that you buy when you pay that all-inclusive fee. Arguably, 'community-as-a-service' is oxymoronic – after all, when it comes to community, don't you only get out what you put in? One of the issues with community is the moral baggage that surrounds it,[25] which can lead to the kind of judgemental statements like the one I just made. What counts as 'authentic' community? (What does that even mean?) And can a company with a profit motive – shock, horror! – ever create or facilitate such a thing? We are right to question it, though at the same time, it is easy to be so sceptical as to become closed-minded.

Within coliving there are some evidenced examples of social connection,[26] much of which comes from research done by coliving operators (who, we cannot ignore, have an incentive to foreground the positive elements of what they're doing). Israeli/American coliving operator Venn[27] found that their resident's loneliness levels dropped by 50% six months after moving in, and that 100% of Venn residents felt socially supported.[28] Spanish operator Urban Campus reported that 85% of their residents felt 'less alone'

22 Lind, D. (2020). Brave New Home: Our Future in Smarter, Simpler, Happier Housing. UK: Hachette, p. 81.

23 ULI (2022) 'ULI and JLL European Coliving Best Practice Guide'. Available at: www.jll.co.uk/en/trends-and-insights/research/the-european-coliving-best-practice-guide (Accessed: 5 March 2023).

24 In itself a vague and highly contested term.

25 White, T. (2022) personal communication, 29 September.

26 Which arguably is a facet of 'community'.

27 Venn has since changed its focus from coliving to property development, operation, and neighbourhood engagement, though at the time of the research cited they were coliving operators.

28 Venn (2019) Semi-annual Impact Report. (Accessed: 5 March 2023) Available at: drive.google.com/file/d/1Z_sDHolYoJBqvo4s2Jbo7TFiG-1sSJNA/view

thanks to their community,[29] and a recent report by a consortium of coliving operators found that residents felt closer to their neighbours as a result of coliving.[30] These findings are captured by a review of French operator, Vitanovae: "I was pretty depressed when I moved into the Triplex. I had just gotten divorced in Paris and for the first few months, I often stayed alone in my studio. The other residents, younger than me, really supported me. They opened my eyes and even allowed me to meet my current partner."[31] Beyond research from operators, there are currently few studies which explore community or social connection in coliving. A nuanced, small-scale study of a large coliving space found that the elements of community (defined as identification with place, common ties, and regular social interaction) were reflected to "a certain extent", with common ties between residents being the most difficult to identify. The researcher found that residents' views, experiences and levels of satisfaction differed widely[32] (an indication that if we want straightforward answers when it comes to community, we are unlikely to find them). One further small-scale study was more positive. Researchers interviewed twelve residents of a digital nomad community, and found that coliving "creates countless opportunities for human connection and friendships to flourish", and that residents were "able to form a fluid community", with users being able to "join in and leave based on their personal schedule and also the rules of each co-living space".[33] Whilst there is some evidence of coliving mitigating loneliness and enabling social connections, there is still a gap to explore as to what 'community' in coliving means, and whether the industry is, on the whole, achieving its promise.

The above study, which refers to a community where residents can "join in and leave" more or less as they like, speaks to the concept of 'community-as-a-service'. Community, with much of the work taken out: no cleaning rotas, no dealing with splitting bills, meetings and events that you know will still happen if you

29 Urban Campus (2022) 'New Coliving Report 2022'. Available at: urbancampus.com/es/blog/nuevo-coliving-report-2021/ (Accessed: 5 March 2023).

30 Worldwide Coliving Membership (2023) 'Flexible Living Trend Report 2023 Vol. 1'. Available at: www.epsd.co.kr/en/wcm/ (Accessed: 5 March 2023).

31 Conscious Coliving (no date) 'Conscious Coliving Projects'. Available at: www.consciouscoliving.com/projects/ (Accessed: 5 March 2023).

32 Hocking, A.E.M. (2020) 'Community is the answer, but what was the question?'. Masters Thesis. Cambridge University.

33 Von Zumbusch, J.S.H. and Lalicic, L. (2020) 'The role of co-living spaces in digital nomads' well-being', Information Technology & Tourism, 22(3), pp.439-453.

don't show up, and that you can dip in and out of when you want to. In her book, *Living Together*, Mim Skinner visits London-based Mason & Fifth and finds what appears to be genuinely happy and harmonious residents. A former resident tells her: "It wasn't fake, what you saw [...] It's a really lovely place to live. Everyone really is that nice, all the time. Of course they are. It's easy to be nice when you're rich and everything is being done for you."[34] It's common for coliving operators to speak the language of personal growth, and to offer it in the form of professional development classes, wellness practices and coaching. However, there is a notable silence on the potential for the personal growth that comes from living with others. I have heard (and witnessed the eyerolls of) numerous coliving staff commenting that residents expect them to solve their interpersonal problems, such as noisy neighbours. But, to indicate that coliving residents are simply pampered customers is far too glib and simple. Anecdotally, I have also seen that it's not uncommon for residents to run events or arrange outings, and operators have shared with me that they have facilitated group discussions to help solve interpersonal difficulties (personal growth with a helping hand). It is also common for operators to offer socially impactful volunteering opportunities, which enables neighbourhood integration, and for many residents, may be their first experience of volunteering for social causes (Venn found that their residents' volunteering rates doubled after six months of living there[35]). The point still stands that within coliving, much of the 'work' of community living (whether physical, intellectual or emotional) is delegated to service providers, and with that, certain opportunities for personal growth are diluted or lost. Yet, for money-rich, time-poor individuals, coliving offers an accessible version of community, which, in my view, is a significant improvement on renting a studio or one-bed and living alone.

Having said that, it is worth noting that there is a knowledge gap in the sector, and that sometimes, the biggest commitment that coliving operators show to community is on the landing page of their website! The fact that community is mentioned so prominently and frequently shows that operators perceive it has value to potential customers. However, until there is more research which proves the business case for commu-

34 Skinner, M. (2022) Living Together. London: Footnote, pp.87-88.
35 Venn (2019) Semi-annual Impact Report. (Accessed: 5 March 2023) Available at: drive.google.com/file/d/1Z_sDHoIYoJBqvo4s2Jbo7TFiG-1sSJNA/view

nity, and more understanding of best practice[36] there is a risk of 'community-washing', or "faux-living".[37] The former point about the business case is key: an operator deciding how much resources to put into facilitating community has to view things through the lens of profitability, which inevitably shapes their actions. Every community must act within the bounds of their resources, nevertheless, things look different when the goal is ultimately to make a financial profit.

Profitability comes into play even more apparently when looking at room sizes in coliving, with a clear financial incentive to have as many people as possible living in as small a space as possible. The fear of inadequate private space has fed into more than one planning rejection in the UK.[38] It is a legitimate concern, and this pressure, along with evidence of resident preferences, has led to room sizes trending upwards, with proposed schemes tending to have studios in the 20-25 sqm range[39] – still modest, but a far cry from the well known experiment in coliving which was The Collective Old Oak, which had units as small as 12 sqm. What constitutes enough private space is a complex question which extends beyond a measuring tape. Part of the answer lies in how comfortable the resident feels in the communal spaces, which is linked to the type and quality of those spaces, the quality of social connections they have with other users of those spaces, and – of course – their personal attributes and preferences. Satisfying private spaces also depends more on the feeling of spaciousness, rather than the amount of space,[40] and the coliving sector has produced some impressive examples of well-designed, compact studios.[41] High quality but compact homes are important given our growing population and the urgent need for environmentally sustainable housing.

36 See: 'The Community Facilitation Handbook', www.consciouscoliving.com/the-community-facilitation-handbook (Accessed: 5 March 2023).

37 See 'The Faux-living Manifesto', www.faux-living.info (Accessed: 5 March 2023).

38 See: Robson, S. (2020) 'The shared 'co-living' flats with such small bedrooms they could trigger a Manchester crackdown'. Manchester Evening News, 11 January; and Whelan, D. (2022) 'Crosslane loses Liverpool co-living appeal', Place North West, 20 September.

39 Savills (2022) 'Spotlight: UK Co-living – a market poised for huge growth. Available at: www.savills.co.uk/research_articles/229130/328949-0 (Accessed: 4 March 2023).

40 The Happiness Research Institute and Kingfisher Plc (2019) 'The GoodHome Report'. (Accessed: 5 March 2023) Available at: www.happinessresearchinstitute.com/publications/the-goodhome-report-

41 For examples, see: Cutwork's 'Polyroom', for NOMO coliving, based in France (cutworkstudio.com/polyroom-by-bouygues-immobilier); and European operator Zoku's 'Lofts' (livezoku.com/amsterdam/stay/).

Densification is part of the answer to making our homes more sustainable,[42] and coliving, through its mix of minimal private space and larger shared communal areas, could offer a best-of-both-worlds solution at scale.

Communal dining room at Zoku, Amsterdam

Studio with mezzanine bed at Zoku, Amsterdam

This ability to scale is both a strength and a risk. Grassroots communal living projects (e.g. cohousing) are rare, and usually their conception is the result of extremely dedicated volunteers who are both hard-working and fortunate. Coliving, as a professional endeavour, does not face the same barriers, and as an industry has the expertise and can attract the capital to build rapidly, at scale. Coliving is therefore bringing the idea of aspirational communal living to a wider group of people, offering an alternative view on what a good home looks like, and potentially acting as a 'gateway' to a more collaborative view of the world.[43] Yet, scale is also antithetical to the forming of community, as it detracts from sensitivity to place and intimacy with

2 Pauliuk, S., Heeren, N., Berrill, P., Fishman, T., Nistad, A., Tu, Q., Wolfram, P. and Hertwich, E.G., (2021) 'Global scenarios of resource and emission savings from material efficiency in residential buildings and cars', Nature communications, 12(1), pp.1-10.

3 A common phrase in the coliving industry is that people 'come for the convenience and stay for the community'.

people, and there are important questions being asked about if and how architectural, interior, operational and social design can mitigate these impacts.

Coliving is communal living through a commercial lens, and ultimately will always be shaped by a profit motive. With this in mind, a question to consider is to what extent a profit motive can be aligned with social and environmental good? The answer to this question is wrapped up in broader contexts around regulatory environments, non-mandatory business best practice and norms (e.g. sustainability certifications), customer expectations, and the values of those in the business and up and down supply chains.

Not too long ago, I helped to moderate a panel where three coliving operators were guest speakers. I was struck by how different they were. The first ran a boutique rural coliving space, talked about the importance of shared values, and said that she was exploring having a tiny house village on the land. The second was a manager of a building with just over 200 rooms, and one of the things she talked about was her approach to community and creating great resident experiences. The third was an ex-CEO of a very large operator, who said that they had a target to scale to 4000-5000 rooms and seek further investment. Three different scales, and different possibilities for what coliving looks like. Let's see what emerges from the sector in the coming years.

Communal area at Zoku Amsterdam

Dr Penny Clark
is a shared living researcher, Diggers and Dreamers board member, and Co-Founder of Conscious Coliving, a research and consultancy company which helps embed social and environmental impacts within coliving.

The Meaning of Community at L'Arche

LUCILLE KENNEDY, NEM TOMLINSON, LOUISE DETAIN AND CHRIS ASPREY

Three stories describe how – through living together – people with and without learning disabilities come to understand and appreciate one another.

Founded in France in 1964, L'Arche is a network of more than 150 Communities in 37 countries, where people with and without learning disabilities share life together[1]. There are 11 Communities in the UK. Community members include people with learning disabilities (often referred to as L'Arche's "core members"), assistants who provide support and care, as well as a wider network of friends, volunteers and local neighbours. L'Arche seeks to combine a community experience with commissioned and regulated care provision for people with disabilities. The heart of L'Arche Communities lies in the transformative potential of the friendships and mutual relationships that are built across diversity and difference.

The three stories in this chapter are testimony to these relationships, and to the freedom, authenticity and fullness of life they contain. The chapter concludes with a reflection on what makes these relationships an experience of community.

Jenny's Vocation

Lucille Kennedy reflects on how Jenny, a core member in the L'Arche Preston Community, is gifted at ensuring people are not lost at the edges of our society and are seen as human beings.

Not to be confused with the spiritual commune of the same name, founded by Lanza del Vasto in southern France in 1948

Four years ago I embarked on a research project for a Masters in Health Psychology. I had just read a PhD paper by Jani Klotz. Three of her siblings were labelled with severe and profound learning disabilities. Reading Jani's paper opened my eyes to some of the ways we value our community members in L'Arche and provided a new language to express the importance of their lives. As a result, it led me to conduct a piece of inclusive research with four of our community members in Preston. Jenny was one of them.

In her paper, Jani mused on one of the important things her sister spends time doing – collecting tiny bits and pieces from her environment and carrying them around with her. At night she would spread the bits and pieces out on her bed in a particular order. This was something she had always done but, when she left her parents' home to live in a group house, this behaviour was labelled as obsessive compulsive and seen as unhealthy (as it also seemed to cause some soreness in her hand).

To address this, her care team decided to control Jani's sister's access to her bits and pieces, and insist she carry them around with her in a small purse. The family was instructed that they must also be consistent with this regime when she visited them. Jani ignores the instruction. She doesn't understand what it is her sister is doing, but she knows it is something of great importance to her. She recounts seeing the deep contentment in her sister when she has settled down in bed with her bits and pieces ordered around her. She feels it is her sister's vocation to do this.

Her sister's vocation? This struck a deep chord with me when I thought about all my friends in L'Arche who engage in behaviours that we don't understand, and may try to control, but which are crucial to their individual well-being.

While I was reading about Jani's sister, the television was on in front of me showing the diving competition at the Commonwealth Games. Men and women spend huge amounts of time every day climbing up a ladder and onto a diving board to jump off in one way or another. They do this over and over again. It is completely pointless, but they get really, really good at it by doing it all the time. They win medals for doing this.

This set me thinking about why we value some repetitive behaviours and yet pathologise other behaviours as

Jenny

obsessive compulsive. What is it that drives the desire to do something, even when others try to prevent it, or make it difficult? How is this linked to our vocation and why each of us was created?

So let's hear from Jenny; a wonderful and amazing woman who lives in L'Arche Preston.

Jenny likes to carry a disposable plastic bag, which contains papers of one sort or another. Anyone who knows Jenny will know how important her bag of papers is to her. Sometimes the papers are raffle tickets, sometimes envelopes, or flyers. Jenny's focus throughout the day is to keep this collection safe and she will spend time ordering and organising it. How is this related to Jenny's vocation?

To explore this question, the two of us met for a couple of hours a week for a six-week period and played with paper. I brought coloured paper, shiny paper, holographic paper, textured paper, notebooks, folders, envelopes and a scrap book. I collected magazines and brought pens, glue, scissors and some shaped punches. I put all this stuff on the table and sat with Jenny to see what happened.

One of the things Jenny made a beeline for were the shaped punches. Jenny loved using them and cut out many shapes. She put the shapes very carefully into a folder, ensuring none were lost. I started to gather all the bits of paper from which the shapes had been cut, to throw away. Jenny showed signs of distress at this point and it became clear that it was important to her to keep the 'relief' of the shape also, so all the bits of paper went into the folder for safety.

This was a real 'a-ha' moment for me as I realised that Jenny wanted to rescue all the things that I throw away. To her these are of value. All the things that Jenny carries around with her are things I treat as valueless. I began to see Jenny's precious bag of paper more like a piece of artwork, like Tracey Emin's 'My Bed'; something visual which makes a statement about contemporary society.

During the six weeks we worked together, there was a regional community gathering. At the gathering there was a young man, Thomas, and his parents, who were exploring L'Arche as a place for Thomas to live. Thomas has profound and multiple disabilities and was, therefore, the person in the room most vulnerable to exclusion. Jenny sat next to him. At one point in the conversation, Thomas' parents were talking about going away for the weekend.

Jenny immediately began to display the same anxiety that she showed when we missed rescuing a piece of paper from the floor and she said to Thomas' parents: 'You are going to take Thomas with you, aren't you?' This was the moment that I realised that Jenny wasn't just alert to paper being lost, but was in fact aware of anything and anyone who may be lost at the edges and may be vulnerable to being 'thrown away'. In our last session we stuck all of Jenny's work into a scrapbook. This included all the paper she had cut and many pictures that she had chosen to cut out from magazines. This meant that I had a body of work on which I could carry out a thematic analysis. One of the striking things I noticed when looking at Jenny's scrapbook was how it was full of pictures of women. The only picture of a man in the entire scrapbook was a tiny picture of Barry Norman's head. Jenny likes men, many of her friends are men, her dad is her great hero, but in her world it is women who she notices doing the important things and women's work that she values.

Jenny's scrapbook containing images of women. In Jenny's world, it is women who she notices doing valuable work

After I had given birth to my son Gabriel, I was on maternity leave and one evening when at L'Arche Preston Jenny said to me: 'You're working with Gabriel tomorrow, are you?' I nearly wept at Jenny's recognition of what I was doing as a mother, in a culture which regards full-time motherhood as not working.

In the same way that Tom Daley can do extraordinary things between leaving the diving board and hitting the water, Jenny is also extraordinary in her abilities to spot and act on exclusion and marginalization. Jenny hones her skills and expertise all the time, noticing what and who is vulnerable to being lost at the edges, excluded, or thrown away. She then acts on this in her own determined way, challenging the rest of us to see our world and our values in a new light.

Is this why Jenny has been put on this earth? Is this her vocation? I think it is.

Lucille Kennedy
first joined L'Arche Liverpool in 1982 and was a founder member of L'Arche Preston. From 2016-2022, she was a member of L'Arche in Brecon, but is now back in Preston working part time for the national team and supporting her 7 children and 14 grandchildren.

When I'm at L'Arche I like my body

Nem Tomlinson is part of the L'Arche Manchester Community, which she co-founded in 2013.

I came to L'Arche when I was 22. I was straight out of university and I celebrated my 23rd birthday just weeks later. My housemates baked me a cake, fumbled thank yous and gifted me slippers (they didn't know me well enough then to know that I tolerate shoes at the best of times. I still have those slippers – unworn. They remind me that I am loved). For the last ten years I have been woven into the L'Arche Community in Edinburgh and, for the last six years, here in Manchester. I have grown up in L'Arche; for better, for worse, for richer, for poorer, in sickness and in health. I have lived my greatest joys and my deepest shames amidst my communities, and they have been the contexts and often the sources of my healing; the messy, ugly putting oneself back together that inevitably happens with life.

At university I wrote my undergraduate dissertation on naked Quaker women and my Masters dissertation on the function of seventeenth century breasts. Before L'Arche, and during my studies, I spent a lot of time thinking about what having a body meant and perhaps less time thinking about what my body meant to me. This changed when I joined L'Arche. Life in L'Arche is an embodied experience. There are baths to run, teeth to brush, feet to massage, arms to link. There are shared, noisy meal times where we join hands to sing, and impromptu dance parties as we wash up. There is signing to tell a story: the one that happened long before she moved in, but that we all know and tell, and tell again, fingers moving to share it with someone new. I do less of this now and I still miss it, sneaking it in whenever I can.

Embodiment is a term that is slowly becoming more recognised. It has taken time because we are, largely, a society that values the head and intellect over the body, it seems. For me, embodiment describes the process of locating myself within myself (all of me, my body), and in the present moments. Body Positivity is a movement that espouses the idea that all bodies are good. Yet having a body can be a complex thing. Loving other people's bodies has been a much simpler process for me than loving my own.

I can tell you about our core members in Manchester. How Milly has eyelashes that could launch a thousand ships, or what it does to my heart when Crispin giggles and twitches with delight. I can tell you about helping Joe to have a shave in the morning, listening to Herb Albert, and how the process would take twice as long because we would dance as he shaved. I can tell you of the process of falling in love with people time and time again. But my relationship with loving this body I inhabit has not always been simple. I would struggle to tell you what I find precious about it, and could tell you how I have hated it and hurt it and shamed it.

Embodiment has given me a language to explore the idea that there is no separation between me and my

Nem

body. We are all me. But it is in L'Arche that I've learnt what embodiment feels like and perhaps feeling might be the key to embodiment.

R.S. Thomas has a line in his poem, The Kingdom, which reads '...and love looks at them back.' I think so often that this has been my experience within L'Arche. Lou doesn't care how much I weigh; she cares about whether we will talk about the time I forgot to pick her up from her nana's, and arrived sweaty and beetroot red from a run.

In the autumn I dyed my hair green impulsively and Zeynep tugged at it and screeched with delight. Crispin and I twirl at our Community Boogie Nights, and I feel free and alive. Milly pumps her arm up and down with unabashed joy and grabs your clothing as you pass her, so that you stop and bend down to share a joke with her.

It is not our differences that have taught me peace with my own body. It is not some misplaced, harmful, platitude along the lines of 'if they are happy with their bodies, I should be happy with mine.' No. Rather, it is that in their loving me, they have taught me that I am good; all of me. The embodied me is good.

People tease me about when I last brushed my hair. It is speckled with grey. The laughter lines that started ten years ago in a three-storey house in Leith where this story began are now embedded in my skin. I throw on clothes in the morning and rarely think about what I look like. I have started to think less and less often about what I look like. Instead I am learning to understand my life by asking myself: 'what do I feel like?'

So when Lou and I, after many false starts, climb up the stairs on the water flume for the eighth time and slide belly laughing all the way down, I feel like I am eight years old again and riding my bike. When Zeynep runs towards me with arms wide open, I know that I am good. When Crispin jumps up when I knock on his front door, and raises his arms and dances from side to side, I know I belong.

This hard-earned friendship that says 'you are important to me and me to you.' Mary Oliver wrote 'You only have to let the soft animal of your body love what it loves.' This simple revolution. To ask what does this beat up, broken and put-back-together body of mine love? A work of a lifetime; learning to listen and love and inhabit myself.

I am learning this in L'Arche. Most of the people who I share my life with don't speak, but they don't need to. They tell me who they are and what they want in a myriad of different and deep ways, and they tell me that I am their friend and that they love me in embodied ways. 'Love looks at me back' each day and because of that I am learning to centre myself within myself. To twirl and twirl and dance, hot and sweaty and imperfect, and know that this is good.

When I'm at L'Arche I like my body and, because of that, I am learning to love it when I'm not.

Nem Tomlinson
is currently the Community Leader of L'Arche Manchester which has been her place of belonging since 2012. She began her life in L'Arche in 2008 as part of the Edinburgh Community.

The importance of being known

Louise Detain is a founding member of the L'Arche Community in Nottingham.

When she was 21, Louise left her job and lived for a year as part of the L'Arche community in Ipswich. Here she found something remarkable in a community where people can love well, and disagree well, and live together well.

Being a part of L'Arche has prepared her for many aspects of her life: for parenthood, for her career, and for fostering children. She, her partner and their daughter (pictured) are now members of L'Arche in Nottingham.

One of the really important things that I found L'Arche has to offer is being known. I mean being known not by what we do or what we can bring, but actually just who we are. I think so often people with learning disabilities become 'paper', in a sense. They have a lot of systems that organise their lives for them and everything is reviewed and monitored and evaluated. But actually L'Arche, in its essence, puts importance in the human – in addition to all of the other things that have to happen.

But also as a person without a learning disability life can be really lonely. I think particularly having had a baby, it's wonderful to be involved in a community that loves my children, but also who give them so much and give me so much. It's meant that on maternity leave when typically a lot of people find themselves very isolated, actually I haven't. I have found myself more surrounded by people that I love because they're so invested in our family.

I've learnt more from my friends with learning disabilities than I have from many, many others. I've learnt to be more patient, I've learnt to be more gentle. It's prepared me for lots of different parts of my life: for parenthood, for lots of my jobs. If it hadn't been for some of the people with learning disabilities that I have befriended I would have been really rubbish at lots of those jobs. I've also learnt how to laugh more and how to have more joy.

Louise

I was on my way to the Christmas community gathering this evening thinking that nothing had gone right today at all. It's been one of those days where I've missed everything that I was supposed to do. I was driving and I couldn't remember if I had left the oven on and it was just a bit of a mess. I was starting to think 'I can't be bothered to go. It's such an effort. Why have I had such a rubbish day? Nothing's gone to plan. I've not done anything I was supposed to do and I'm late for this too.'

And then I walk in and I'm instantly loved. I had said to myself on the way here: 'Even if I didn't go, no one would notice.' But actually I know people would. And there aren't many places in my life where I know if I didn't turn up to a big gathering like this, people would notice. Tonight we have noticed who isn't here. We notice that about each other. And we notice because we are special to one another and because we love one another.

Louise Detain
is a member of L'Arche Nottingham, first came to L'Arche in Ipswich in 2006. Motivated by their experiences and sense of belonging in L'Arche, Louise and her wife Caireen became foster carers in 2011 providing long term security to a child in the care system.

In what sense is L'Arche a community experience?

L'Arche member Chris Asprey reflects upon what community means at L'Arche.

The heart and soul of L'Arche is found in relationships that cut across all sorts of differences. That is the common theme in each of the three stories in this chapter. It is a perspective that shifts what we have often understood community to be, both inside and outside L'Arche.

One of the first theorists of community, Ferdinand Tönnies, introduced into sociology a distinction between community (Gemeinschaft) and society (Gesellschaft). What he had in mind were two contrasting ways in which human beings tend to associate with each other.

Community associations, Tönnies thought, are the natural, spontaneous, effortless bonds, which emerge when two or more people are united by a shared understanding. That kind of association is organic, and hardly requires effort or negotiation to create or maintain it. Tönnies thought that close family and sexual ties, experienced in the life of the home, were the primary archetypes for community, followed by local neighbourhoods and friendships. By contrast, he thought of society as a set of artificial and unnatural transactions, such that social relationships would collapse altogether if they weren't sustained by repeated effort and individual choice.

People who visit a L'Arche home, where a small mixed group of people with and without disabilities live together, often see the hallmarks of organic community. In L'Arche households, community is forged through the shared rhythms of daily life: the preparing and sharing of meals, patterns of rest and work, sharing the household chores, catching up with each other at the end of the day, times of prayer or reflection. In shared living, rituals of belonging begin to emerge quite spontaneously, becoming habitual in a household and starting to shape the way collectively we think, feel and behave.

That phenomenon is expressed in the words of L'Arche's 1993 Charter: "Home life is at the heart of a L'Arche Community." The statement matches Tönnies' view that the closest analogy to community is the family bond. Moreover, in earlier decades, this belief was reflected in various ways, including our commitment to pay everyone equally, whatever their role or level of responsibility.

Things have changed today. We operate in a more regulated social care environment, where salary structures and pay scales are the norm. Of the 11 L'Arche Community sites in the UK, 10 employ assistants to provide commissioned and regulated social care. We have had to keep pace with the 2014 Care Act, and the disability movement as a whole, by making individual choice paramount in the way we support people with learning disabilities in L'Arche. Time is divided into work time and free time, a distinction driven by the ideology of market society, not the organic cycles of community. Spending my free time with someone with a learning disability becomes a matter of personal choice rather than a collective habit.

In reality, however, community in L'Arche has never been and could never be entirely organic, natural, spontaneous and effortless. Anyone who joins a L'Arche Community is quickly immersed in difference: people of different backgrounds, nationalities, faiths, sexualities, abilities, outlooks on life, ways of communicating. And negotiating such differences always involves challenge and hard work.

Our identity statement describes L'Arche as "people with and without learning disabilities, sharing life". The statement asserts L'Arche as a single body. However, it immediately names two groups, not only distinct from each other, but defined as opposites: with and without. That opposition reflects the ableist prejudice that people with learning disability are essentially "other" than the rest of us.

L'Arche's mission is to overcome that bias, but doing so is not straightforward. Because our world marginalises learning disability – and many people have never so much as met someone with a learning disability before – the encounter between people with and without disabilities is almost never frictionless. This is as true in L'Arche as it is elsewhere, but in L'Arche we are committed to confronting the challenge.

Today, our new Charter (it is currently still in draft form) will define community in looser terms, as a "network of relationships". It is these relationships, rather than life within the home, that best describes community in L'Arche. The home continues to be important, of course. It is the place where many relationships in L'Arche are forged. However, we are increasingly attuned to the ways community is meaningful for people in and around L'Arche, who are not necessarily living together under one roof.

So, community in L'Arche is above all a network of relationships which cut across our differences, as the stories in this chapter illustrate. Its hallmarks are genuine mutuality, combined with the challenge and transformative potential of meeting each other in our differences and working them through. These mutual relationships are the founding experience and guiding insight of L'Arche, both within the community home and outside it.

Community at l'Arche

Chris Asprey
is a member of the L'Arche Community in London and head of communications for L'Arche in the UK. He previously lived in a L'Arche community in northern France.

London Street Commune

SUPERCREW

The Voice of Communal Living Past. Vintage squatter Supercrew chronicles the highs and lows of the "Dilly Dossers".

The London Street Commune was a very loose knit affair and it certainly shouldn't be thought of as an organised urban movement in any sense of the term. For the previous couple of years a group of young hippies (and that is the last time I shall use that naff, tabloid generated term... we were Freaks!) had made Piccadilly Circus their home. There were around 20 or so of us who would be considered hardcore. We were always there, always around, we knew all the good hustles that could be had in Soho and its environs and in those days it was easy to live on the streets.

Covent Garden was still a fruit'n'veg market and the produce was there for the picking up; no one minded once it had fallen off a trolley, a sort of unwritten rule, if it was on the floor it was fair game. The Wardour Street bakery was thriving and always produced a supply of bread and cakes for the asking. Busking pitches were uncrowded. Freaks were a new phenomenon and many curious people wanted to engage us in conversation which was usually good for a touch. The Sally Ann (Salvation Army) were down on the Embankment and if you got really stuck there was always the Crypt under St Martins but few of us ever resorted to those last two mentioned.

We reckoned the West End was ours and tried to get away with as much as we could... no one was truly dishonest in a damaging sort of way but we did enjoy with revolutionary zeal the liberating of many a choice item from the clutches of the grey establishment types that ran the Oxford Street emporiums. We obstructed the pavement around the Pronto coffee bar on the east side of Piccadilly Circus as we tried to flog the precursor of *The Big Issue, International Times (IT)* magazine to suited and bowler hatted clerks on their way to and from the office, and acted up a bit for the tourists in that great old tradition known as 'freaking out the straights'. We were a friendly and colourful bunch but also a trifle loud and smelly and the powers that be took an increasing dislike to our presence in the tourist centre of the British Empire (foundered).

Although there were some junkie types on the fringes of the 'Dilly Dossers', as we were known, the majority of us only used dope and acid, and surprisingly enough in hindsight I don't remember much alcohol consumption past a couple of beers and those infrequently. We were a pretty harmless lot really but that's not quite how the authorities viewed us. Stop and search by the police was for us a daily occurrence and it was generally conducted in reasonable politeness by the officers concerned once it had been established that we were not about to scream 'Off the Pigs' in their faces. Actually we used to call them Fuzz... the term Pigs came over from the States in the early seventies.

Gradually though we came under increased pressure to vacate our beloved Dilly. The tabloid press suddenly decided that we were fair game with *The News of the World* publishing a centre spread of us sitting on the Dilly steps under the headline: "Everyone in this picture is a degenerate or a junkie".

Every summer our nucleus of 20 or so was swollen by the influx of those we used to term 'weekend ravers'. Those were kids still living with their parents who would escape and come and live on the Dilly with us over the weekends. We were their heroes and we shamelessly took advantage of that fact by selling them bum deals, borrowing money and stealing their girlfriends... sorry guys. In addition to these folks there were also visitors to Britain who found our lifestyle attractive and hung around with us, often for weeks or even months at a time.

We didn't live in squats in those days, we lived in 'derrys'. Slang for derelict houses of which there were thousands in the sixties. They had a certain short life and when the bulldozers moved in we moved on.

For a lot of early 1969 we had been living in a derry down on the Queenstown Road just over Chelsea Bridge and had become close friends with the bikers that hung out around the all night café by there. We were, however, not on good terms with crowds of football fans and/or skinheads. One particular night of clashes cemented our friendship with the Windsor Angels bikers. We were partying and a large crowd of 'skulls' came by for a ruckus. After some fairly desperate fights occurred, lots of the skinheads ended up dragged off by the Fuzz, who that evening left us alone. So did the skinheads who never returned.

The police dispersed and the party went on well into the night. When we were finally laid back with a spliff in the derry we felt a real power inside us and – if asked – I would say that that night was a bit of a catalyst for us Dilly dossers... suddenly we had achieved something and we felt the strength of a coherent group. Previously we had gone to the offices of *The News of the World* and the *The People* to complain about the articles and of course had been rebuffed. But this time we had confronted and overcome, albeit on a basic physical level. I think it was probably the very first real kickstart of the idea that shortly became the London Street Commune (LSC).

We got very cocky over this victory and the authorities took due note and responded. They started sending council workers to regularly wash down the steps of the Dilly with fire hoses. This always happened in the late evening when the steps would be most crowded and the workmen had obviously received instructions to have a bit of fun. They would happily bowl over anyone who didn't move smartly out of the way or amuse themselves by directing the hoses at any unattended baggage or guitar.

We got our own back but it cost us dearly in the end. On the top step of the Dilly there is a large manhole. It leads deep into the depths of the fountain to where the pumps are located. So one night we watched for their arrival and took the manhole cover off to make a kind of pitfall trap. I don't think the workman was seriously injured, his hose stopped him falling all the way to the floor but it sure did piss a whole lot of people off.

After that the pace hotted up. The workmen would now arrive with a police escort who cleared us from the Dilly and surrounds, chivvying us into side streets or arresting us for obstruction. The daily stop and searches became even more frequent and we were violently removed from the derry in Battersea and ended up down the Worlds End with a very long walk each day to Sloane Square tube. The tubes were our travel lines... there were still loads of stations where entry or exit went unnoticed if you knew the back stair routes and we certainly knew them all.

It must have been around the time of the big skinhead fight, or just after, when Phil arrived on the Dilly. I don't know who gave him the title of Doctor John or why but he didn't have it when he arrived... he was Phil. I think I only remember his last name because of the subsequent publicity but he was in some ways a little different to us, he didn't dress in freak's clothing for example, scruffy as anything but with a worn suit jacket and mismatched trousers. When we were all sporting loons and cheesecloth with beads he always looked the wild bearded student bit. He was certainly into Agitprop, Tariq Ali, Che and all that stuff, whereas we were more inclined to skin-up and see if we could get the Dilly record shop to play Jefferson Airplane on its outdoor speakers.

He was around and part of the first group of us who mooted the idea of the LSC and it was certainly him that became our spokesperson and our face. Just as well really. We would have been more inclined to tell the media to piss off rather than see that there was a certain way to manipulate these things. I'm not saying Phil was successful in his handling of the media but he had more of a clue than the rest of us.

As I said, the pressure was growing on us and we felt we had to make some kind of stance. One night someone, I can't remember who, came up with the LSC idea. If we could create a sensible group maybe we could get help against what we saw as police harassment and public approbation, not to mention getting fed up with being moved around from stinking derry to stinking derry whenever the police got bored enough to conduct a dawn raid. All might have faded into a stoned miasma once again if it hadn't been for the Pronto bar.

That poor business had suffered from us blocking its door, taking hours over one cup of coffee, generally hanging out without spending a penny and occupying valuable seating space that should have been reserved for paying customers. When the owner, in exasperation sold what should have been a goldmine the new owners took immediate and drastic action. They banned us! I don't blame them... In retrospect I would have banned us but there ya go.

We were furious, we were better organised than before because we had BADGES... we all had these naff red cardboard badges with LSC and a black stripe... very anarchist. This was the time of the big sit-ins, and Phil was the one who said, 'OK let's have a Pronto bar sit-in'. So we did... for hours, and we ate all the food and thought we were jolly brave and revolutionary and all that guff but really it was a joke that those poor owners didn't deserve. But for us it was another bit of direct action that placed the power in our hands... we even had a slogan for the LSC which started going up as graffiti... The London Street Commune Fights Back The Fuzz NOW...

It's been a long time and dates are out of the loop but it was shortly after the Pronto bar that we heard about the squats out at Redbridge, and that seemed like the answer to our housing problems. But instead of squatting in the leafy suburbs we remembered that we were kids of the Dilly and took for our first squat Broad Court slap bang next to Bow St Magistrates Court, in fact so close that on several occasions messengers arrived from Number 1 Court asking us if we minded keeping the noise down.

Broad Court was a curious corner building, not very high but made up of a warren of small rooms, silly ground floor sash windows that yielded instantly to Coventry Johnny's thin blade and we were in with no damage... warm, dry, with glass in the windows! Man this was living for us who had been used to rude awakenings as thieves stripped the piping and lead from over our very heads or hacked through a water main to flood us out.

Then everything changed again.

Jude and I had been together for three years by that time and were probably seen as an inseparable couple, but we both had our flings when it suited us and in

Broad Court I met Jenny. She and I decided to hitch to somewhere together and found ourselves on the beach in Aberystwyth for a few days. On our return we found things being run on a slightly different footing. Mad Mick had moved in.

Mick was a really nasty piece of work. He and his henchmen were never part of our scene but they were always around our haunts and of course were party to all the news on the street. They had bludgeoned their way into Broad Court, evicted people from the best rooms and set up their headquarters. They were thieves in a very Victorian sense. Pickpocketing, mugging and general extortion and well used to violence.

And why didn't we unite under the LSC banner and collectively evict those bastards? Because we were scared of them. They were a united, motivated, unit with very little brain power between them but nasty enough to do us a lot of damage on an individual level and we knew that if we directly attacked these guys they wouldn't simply melt away like the skinheads. No freak would be safe walking alone in Soho again. So we tried sidestepping them.

Since our first success with Broad Court, scouting parties had been out and about. Endel Street was just around the corner, and right opposite the Oasis Public Baths was a gigantic rambling old church school completely enclosed, with a side alley entrance that was easy to defend. We moved a token group in to secure the premises and printed up the relevant legal documents that explained that squatting was not a criminal offence and that the police had no powers to evict us and had to leave a Civil Court application for eviction to the owners of the property. This was a new area for the police and few understood the laws. We made sure that they were aware of what they could or could not do to us.

At the same time as our holding force was established in Endel Street we sent another much smaller force to 144 Piccadilly and secured that property as well... we then sat back to await results.

By the time Endel Street started our usual summer numbers had almost doubled as word of mouth got around the weekend ravers, who realised that with a secure base they had no real need to go back to Mum and Dad on Sunday night. We started to hear the oft repeated story of 'Hey man, I've given up everything just to be with you guys' and we were getting concerned. This wasn't a joke and we seemed to be becoming the excuse for the year's runaways which wasn't going to go down too well with the tabloids. But for the meantime we'd moved all the more together freaks out of Broad Court and quietly into Endel Street. When Mike's posse turned up at the side door, we apologised profusely but there was simply no room. 'Not to worry though... you've got the whole of Broad Court now'.

That situation didn't last two weeks however before they realised that without our brains and Phil's legal oratory skills they were being thrown to the lions and we awoke one morning to find that some plonker on guard duty had let a bunch of them in and they were now established amongst us again.

It was at that point that we disclosed our occupancy of 144 and reasoned rightly as it turned out that Mad Mick would be content with the two West End squats and wouldn't bother moving off his patch and out to the end of Piccadilly on Hyde Park Corner. Endel Street had been big, with its halls and upstairs chapel but 144 was vast!

We had the main doors facing Hyde Park Corner nailed shut and severely barricaded. The entire property was surrounded by a deep dry moat with sheer sides, so we established a reception room with a drawbridge to the right of the main doors and made sure that whoever was on guard duty was well aware of who was undesirable. Drawbridge sounds pretty posh but in fact it was a sheet of plywood that stretched from the window sill to the top of the moat parapet, around 5 feet high. It was an easy scramble up the parapet and on to the bridge, if it was extended across the void that is.

By now we had given countless newspaper interviews. We had all done some, but Phil was our real spokesman. He was able to talk that student debate talk, emphasising his points with a stabbing finger and sincerity in the eyes behind his thick glasses. This is not a denigration because Phil was a good mate, but the strongest memory I have of him is of sitting around in the mornings in fierce planning get-togethers over breakfast. The breakfast inevitably ended up in Phil's beard, which he never noticed and we never mentioned because we just didn't care, even when we strolled out with him to another rabble of reporters who were kept strictly beyond the iron railings by Curly and his Angel mates. Oh yes we had good security but the next time you see an old cutting of Phil, let me tell ya, that's not spots on the negative, it's probably egg and spliff ash!

We refused all interviews with the tabloids and granted them to only one paper and one film company. I can't remember the name of the film company but every day a van load of milk, bread and other essentials arrived with their compliments and we distributed these as fairly as possible.

Our antics around Broad Court and Endel Street had gained national coverage but it was nothing to the furore created by what was seen as our audacity in taking over 144. This was no back street in WC1, this was a huge ex-embassy in the heart of the establishment, and film crews and reporters were on 24 hour duty outside. The stream of youngsters joining us became a flood even by the first weekend in, and we did voice our concerns to each other and wonder about the sustainability of the whole show, but it was past the point of stopping. We could only have walked away and we were on far too much of a buzz to contemplate that. But I will say we were certainly aware of the potential problems being created although there wasn't much we could do about it... What? Ask freaks to demand proof of age ID off other freaks?... LMFAO (laugh my freaking ass off)!

We didn't do very well when we came up against a proper interviewer either. We were asked by, hhhmm I think it was Thames TV, to appear on the *Today* programme which was hosted live from a studio at the bottom of Kingsway by Eamon Andrews. Phil and around seven or eight of us tromped around and had a very nice cup of coffee and pre-interview chat with good ol' Eamon... You remember him, he used to host the kids show *Crackerjack*, that nice uncle-y sort of geezer.

Over the coffee and studio biccies Eamon asked us lots of questions about our aims and aspirations for a new society. The usual questions came up about free love and flower power. The show was genuinely live with no delay so whatever he chose to say to us we had to respond to and that was that.

It was awful, I remember at one stage he shrugged his shoulders and said 'Well you have no real cause,

you're just a bunch of lazy scroungers aren't you?'
We cringed then and, if I saw it now, I'd cringe again,
but probably laugh the second after. Afterwards we
crawled out knowing full well what dumb idiots we
had appeared. It was bloody embarrassing. Of course
the main problem was that Eamon was basically right
and we all, including Phil knew that.

Some people may choose to remember the LSC as a
motivated alternative group committed to the cause of
freedom but honestly folks... we were a bunch of Dilly
Dossers who were having a whole load of fun. For us
the revolution had landed right on our doorsteps and
we were loving every minute of it. Phil was certainly
the politico of us but he was as much of a space cadet
as Goliath, Franco or anyone else. He had a great way
with words about him and he certainly went on to
some serious altruistic work.

Then came the great skinhead trouncing #2. As I said,
they never returned to the Dilly but one Saturday
afternoon they decided to all come and picnic in the
park and pay us a little visit.

144 Piccadilly was completely empty when we moved
in to it except for one room, a smallish room tucked
behind the lift well, which was full, top to bottom with
sets of multi-coloured boules for some weird reason.
There were hundreds of sets, so thousands of heavy,
solid, perfect hand sized bowls.

The fun started with the skinheads making surges
towards our railings. Our Angels retreated inside,
the drawbridge came up and we were impregnable.
A balcony ran the length of the building on the first
floor and the entire population of 144 assembled on
the battlements. The only thing we had in addition
to the boules was a huge metal tin of ink... someone
produced balloons and several people started throwing
ink filled projectiles.

The skinheads charged the railings, swung around into
the yard, got hit with a hail of boules from above, spun
around to retreat only to find they were now inside
the 8 feet high railings and had to present an exciting sideways moving target as they struggled for the
exits again. That's when I think cars may have been
hit by accident. But to be honest who, in their right
mind, would continue to drive towards a full blown
riot spilling across the north east segment of Hyde
Park Corner... I would have gone round again I think.

The end didn't happen that night... a few days into the week it was... maybe Tuesday? I can't remember and I wasn't there that night, I was at Kenny's over at the Angel. I got the story as I walked down Piccadilly in the morning and met some survivors.

I met up with the crew on the Dilly and this is what happened as everyone I knew confirmed. Remember the runaway kids? Well whatever night it was, it was quiet, the Angels weren't around, someone got lazy and asked a couple of them to mount guard. I bet they were honoured to be asked. But anyway, after a while they were approached by two uniformed cops who told them that they had received a report that a pregnant woman was giving birth inside. They begged that just one of them should be allowed to come in and help her and these plonkers agreed. As soon as the draw-bridge came down it was seized by these two whilst the dozens that had been crouched out of sight below the moat parapet swarmed across and 144 was all over.

The police trashed as much as they could... I don't believe one guitar left that building intact, mine certainly didn't. Everyone was thrown onto the streets as they were. Property that survived the trashing was collected and taken to West End Central Police Station where we glumly queued and gave our names etc till we were reunited with our possessions, in my case the razor slashed remains of mine and Jude's doss bag and a caved-in guitar that would never play again.

That was it, it was all over and that was the end of the LSC.

Shortly after that Jude and I saved a week's busking money and put it down on a room in Belsize Park. Goliath and Sunny came to live with us for a while but we gradually drifted apart. Jude and I got married in 1971. Nobody from the Dilly was there but my mate Kev was my best man. Kev had been on the receiving end of those boules as he and his mates tried to storm us. Funny how life turns ain't it.

Supercrew
went from there to a smallholding in Eire, Backline tech to London's Session Musicians, Tech Director Red Kite Theatre, Married USA County Sheriff, Happily stone carving in the Welsh Marches since.

Still an Option: Squatting in 2023

MICHAEL

Squatting has an important place in the history of housing in Great Britain, and while times (and legislation) have changed since the heyday of the London Street Commune, it's still alive and kicking! Our editor Penny gained a snapshot of squatting today when she spoke with Michael about his experiences of squatting in London.

Penny: Hi Michael, thanks very much for agreeing to speak with me! To start with, it would be great to hear an overview of your experiences of squatting.

Michael: Yeah, sure. So I've been living in squats in London since arriving to the UK in 2011. I first found my way into a squat through meeting people in the punk scene. Shortly after that, I was invited to move into a squat in Chalk Farm in North London. Full of punks, hippies, couch-surfers, rastas... people there were all ages, from their 20s through to mid/late 50s. That's how I first got into the squat scene. Since then I've been involved in various different squats, you know, kind of bohemian housing squats to more hardcore political occupations, and self-organised homelessness shelters as well.

Are you still living in a squat now?

Currently I live in a squat, as with most squats these days, we're there housing ourselves more so than with any other agenda. Yet we're all engaged at least on some level politically and try and make our space available to those who need it. We try to run workshops and meetings occasionally, and ensure that our squat is open to others in moments of crisis such as evictions.

And what was it that drew you to living in squats in the first place?

Yeah, so when I first came to London, I was looking for a place to live, trying to get a job and figure out what I was doing with my life. It wasn't necessarily my plan to stay in London forever, yet here we are 12 years later. But for the time I was here, I wanted to find a community to be part of. Where I'm from there isn't really squatting. But I had lived in punk houses, which, aside from the whole issue of paying rent, may have aesthetically resembled what people might have an impression of a squat to look like. So when I was offered the chance to join, well I knew I wanted to experience and learn more about this squatting situation I had been exposed to.

The lounge, which Michael shares with 10 housemates in London

I think people who haven't experienced squats probably have some stereotyped ideas of what they're like. Could you tell me how the reality compares with some of the stereotypes?

There are various stereotypes, I guess, of what squats look like, and it depends — people's stereotypes will be drawn from their disposition towards the politics of people squatting. To someone who thinks that it's a terrible idea, and doesn't believe in people being able to trespass on private property, well they're more likely to buy into negative stereotypes, you know, "crusties", "crackheads" etc. whatever stories they've been fed. Whereas to someone who has experienced say, political activism around social centres of housing struggles, they might buy into the stereotype that squats are amazing places of organised people that provide communities with spaces and house people.

The reality is that actually squatting is just the act of trespassing to live or to make use of an empty or abandoned property, and in fact all of these things exist. Squatters aren't a homogenous group. My first experience of going into this kind of break-free-of-society utopian house was just one kind of set-up. People squat purely out of necessity, others squat for political reasons etc. For me coming from anarcho-punk houses where like we had gigs in the living room and we organised together to go skipping for food, etc. it wasn't so different from what I was used to. But then over the years, I've been involved in various other things, social centres, housing estate occupations, opening places just to house ourselves without regard to political affiliation, etc., and have seen that all of these things exist concurrently.

Can you tell me a bit about some of the other people you've met and lived with along the way? What have been their circumstances?

Just touching on that first squat I lived in, because I guess it was such a unique experience to walk into... It was roughly a dozen people of all ages and walks of life. So you know, there was anarchist punks, hippies, people wanting to drop out of mainstream society, or perhaps find ways of tearing it down. Other people were couch-surfers who were just looking for an alternative perspective on London while they were there. Other people were let's say, stalwarts of the capital, who had otherwise had previous housing, no longer had access to these kinds of things, for various reasons, and this was the best way that they could house themselves. For all the various situations I've lived in over the years, these days it's not so different.

And how have you coordinated living with others? Do you have certain structures in place for governance, or is it less formal than that?

Again, it's really only the act of trespassing that makes you a squatter. What this means is, at least the idea of what makes a squat is open to the interpretation of people who live in it. So having lived in smaller crews, you know, we've tried to engage in weekly meetings as we currently do now in my current place, trying to ensure practical processes are in place, have structures of care for everyone. And you know I've been in buildings where there's been upwards of 50 people, and it's been a bit of a free-for-all. However people choose to organise themselves within squats... at the end of the day, it's people living with each other, and I would say like the majority of my encounters with that is that people are pretty good at organising themselves to at least to ensure that they've got what they need. The squats where there's been more chaos and less intentional organising has not meant a lack of food on the table. Yeah, so as people live in squats with other people, I think they find the type of people that best suit them and the kind of organising methods that they prefer. And people tend to be pretty free flowing, so you know, people will move about between squats and find who they're most comfortable living with.

In the different places you've lived what's tended to be private and what's tended to be communal?

I guess in most squats that I've lived, things have been pretty anarchic in the sense of ensuring that everyone has everything they need, and then people tend to only privatise personal belongings. Food tends to be shared as with anything that is needed for the continual upkeep of the squat. For example, petty cash, tools, kitchen stuff, things like this. I'm sure that there are people who live in squats that do have a more individual perspective and privatise a lot more, sometimes people might privatise food in the fridge if they for example have a dietary requirement, but it is something of an interesting observation that regardless of background, a lot of people living in squats do tend toward that sense of communal living. Of course, you find out who's got a personal stash once the communal toilet paper runs out.

What have you liked best about squatting?

That's a hard one to answer. At different times, I've appreciated different aspects of living in squats. I guess across all of the different squats, there's always been something special about living with a huge variety of people. Knowing you've all found your way to living in a situation sort of outside of the bounds of regular society, and then utilising that freedom, both in terms of social space and not paying rent to then find common ground and create new ways of living and organising with each other. Obviously, it comes with complications, I like to think of it as a kind of high risk, high reward scenario.

Could you speak a bit more about the challenges and the complications?

Yeah, as much as living with others might be the best thing about squatting, in my experience it can also be the most challenging thing – living with so many people, and trying to ensure everyone's needs are met. Obviously the same goes for anyone that doesn't live on their own, whether that's in private renting or co-ops. We all have to you know, get on with each other if we're to live with each other. I guess there's just something distinct about squatting, that you come across such a diverse range of people with regards to how they've come to squatting, what their needs are. And of course the number of people you tend to live with in squats. There are people that squat on their own for sure, and small squats, but generally I think the average number of people living in a squat is larger than that of your regular housing situation. Once you combine that with the kind of complex needs that arise from what can be a really traumatising living situation, and that sometimes pre-exist leading people to this kind of living situation, I believe it can be harder to resolve or reconcile some of these issues than in other types of housing.

I'm sure you'll know in many intentional communities it's quite common to use certain processes, such as nonviolent communication, for example, or forms of mediation and shared decision-making processes. Have you experienced a similar kind of thing where you've lived?

In places we've definitely engaged in these kinds of processes, meetings, consensus decision making, etc. I think sometimes those types of processes do go somewhat hand-in-hand with the political intention of people. Again, it's down to the people that have chosen to live together, and with squatting, it's so much less homogenous than perhaps other intentional communities. Because for some people, really, it's out of necessity, and not a choice in the same way that other people get together to live, is.

The shared kitchen

Makes sense. And do you have a sense of how squatting has changed over the time you've been involved with it?

Yeah, sure. The most obvious change in the last 11 years is the criminalization of residential squatting. I stepped into squatting just as the LASPO Bill was being pushed through parliament, with Section 144 – the specific part criminalising residential squatting – being snuck in at the 11th hour. Sorry to keep reiterating that squatting's only the act of trespassing and there's no homogenous group to lump people in with, but as far as a "scene" kind of goes, the squats and squatters who shared common ground and wanted to continue these intentional communities... they grew observably fewer and fewer. A lot of people moved into co-ops, onto boats. A lot of events such as workshops, sports etc., that centred around the squatting community started to wind up, as the people who were organising them moved on from squats. This change was evident almost immediately in the wake of 2012. That was more than 10 years ago mind, and the squatting community has been pretty resilient at making do. Like there's been a lot of other attacks, legal and otherwise, on the ability to live in squats. In fact just before speaking to you my own squat was assaulted by owners, bailiffs and police in an attempt to use an old court order to circumvent due process and evict us. Thankfully we're a seasoned lot and we were able to physically resist long enough for someone to get to the high court to have them issue us an order setting aside the old paperwork and helping us wrest back control of our home. And of course we couldn't have done this without massive support from other squats. But anyway despite victories like this I would say it's obvious to most that the average lifespan of the squat is a lot shorter, resulting in a lot more traumatic experiences for people, and you know, a lot more hassle in needing to move on. It also makes it much harder to build upon things that we create in the long-term, moving people's belongings and the spaces they create every couple of months is not conducive to establishing long-term situations. But hey, squatting is admittedly a short-term reality.

However, the need for people to squat never went away. As with any form of punitive judicial bullshit, you can't sweep a "problem" under the carpet and call it a day. Throughout the last 10 years we've still been squatting. There's been massive housing occupations not seen for decades, and we've managed to sustain existing networks and events like workshops, albeit with perhaps less energy and support. Beyond that, people have still simply been getting into abandoned buildings and putting a roof over their heads. That much hasn't changed I reckon. There certainly was a period though that it felt, well, stagnant perhaps. More struggle, less opportunity. However I'd suggest really in the last few years, especially as the system's failed more and more people and as it's shown itself to be the shitshow that it is, that more people are finding their way to squatting, through necessity or interest, and we're starting to see something of a new energy seeking to replace the perceived decline of the last decade. Networks are being revived, restructured, and some even created from new. The last few years have seen autonomous shelters opened to struggle side-by-side with the street homeless populations. There was a run of police stations occupied and used to highlight political grievances against the police as an institution. Squatted community cafes have been opened that have then gone on to form mutual aid groups, the very crux of a lot of support during the COVID crisis. I guess from my limited perspective, squats are now once again being seen, particularly by younger people, as part of the political landscape and not just on the fringes or relics of days-gone-by.

Interesting! And if someone was interested in squatting, what advice would you give to them?

Again it always depends on the circumstances of the person who is in need, or interested in squatting, you know? If a person is in a position to take the time to research their options, then getting in touch with an organisation like the Advisory Service for Squatters would be a good start. London-based, they cover England and Wales, coz the laws in Scotland and Northern Island are different. They've existed for almost 50 years now, started and currently run by other squatters on a purely voluntary basis. They produce the Squatters Handbook, which is a great way to get up to speed with the basics of squatting. It's also likely that there's people at various social centres who either squat or have squatted. Obviously a lot more squatting happens in London than other cities, so it might be harder to find pre-existing squats in other places, but that shouldn't stop anyone I reckon, from just getting out there and getting a roof over their heads. Arm yourself with the enough of the law so as to not put yourself at greater risk than necessary, and go for it!

Why would you say squatting is important?

The fact of the matter is, squatting shouldn't exist. Or rather, the political and economic conditions which makes squatting a necessity shouldn't exist. Access to basic housing and community centres together, etc., have been stripped away, not just over decades, from when people remember "the good old days", but centuries back, as far as the enclosures. And there's people that have always been left in a position where they need or choose to squat. As long as this remains the case, it's imperative that people continue to squat, not only to house themselves and others, but to ensure that everyone's reminded that these conditions exist, and while they do, they will be challenged. There's a saying about this, when talking about "political" squats, that in fact "all squats are political", because of the political and economic conditions that create the need for squatting.

And what would you say to people who say: "It's not your house, what right have you to be there?"

I think the situation depends on who is asking that question, but for me personally it's the arguments of private property, that what right does someone have to leave property empty while people are homeless? It's a status quo that people often don't think to challenge, the notion that private property, it comes before anything else. It's a whole other way of thinking. Even the Human Rights Act enshrines private property as the very first article above all else. Sure, that piece of legislation is meant to protect citizens against governmental interference, but it shows the priority of property over life. I probably shouldn't go into my own view on the ideas of "rights" per se, that might be a bit too much. Anyway, many people like to discuss the idea "how do we solve homelessness"? Yet, people are treated less than private property, so, we're never going to solve this thing so long as we maintain these principles of society.

For what it's worth, the last version of the Squatters Handbook was dedicated to Daniel Gauntlett, a man who died younger than myself, frozen to death outside a long-abandoned house for which he had been threatened with arrest for trying to gain access to only months after the introduction of the residential squatting ban. The law says he deserved to die so that the owners may exercise their right to leave it empty. Fuck that.

Thanks Michael. That's all the questions I have. Is there anything else that you would like to add?

One of the things that I guess was lost somewhere along the way with the repression of squatting is those connections that I've touched on. That there's a political landscape that exists. People may squat for many reasons, and there should never be an expectation for someone who, well, is just putting a roof over their head, but squatting doesn't exist in a void, and is part of a housing struggle which is itself part of a bigger political struggle. This is something I would like to see a return of is, you know, reciprocal support. My experience of some of the co-operatives for example in the UK, they'll say "we like this model of living, but once we've got ours, we're done". OK, they don't actually say that. I'm sure everyone is theoretically sympathetic to other people's situations, and the majority of people I know who live in co-ops are involved in a lot of stuff beyond their own housing. But you know it kind of feels like "housing is no longer our problem" Housing is everyone's problem. I don't want to fall into the trap of stereotypes and slag co-ops off, I've even spent a short time living... and paying rent... in one here. I just think we can all be using our strengths and weaknesses, to support each other.

There were times when it was easier to have squats for years and they were squatted social centres and people would gather in these places. People would share the struggles and it does feel like for the most part, people that are squatting have been left to fend for themselves. It would be great to find ways to rejuvenate that support. I don't have all the answers for that, but it's something I've discussed with people fairly often. I spent time in Greece before the pandemic where my experiences of shared struggle made me feel that this is more important than ever in the squat scene here. Ten years ago for example, when I was relatively new to the squatting community, we set up an eviction resistance network, which was squatters coming together with tenants to try and resist evictions across the board. But it tended to be fairly one way, that is squatters would show up to the evictions of families in the area. Far less support was shown for when a squat was being evicted. Perhaps due to these stereotypes and whatnot that people have. But these attempts have been made and in the past, they have been stronger. We've been involved in occupations of housing estates, fighting alongside tenants that refused to leave, taking space for our own housing and recognising the shared struggle, saying if this is also going to help you and us then this is something worth doing together. Some amazing bonds have been forged through actions like those. But these opportunities have diminished over the years. Yeah, this was, this is something that I would like to see more of. Of course I hark back to the fact that not everyone who is squatting is quote unquote political, but the situation is undeniably so, and it would be good to see squatting be recognised again as part of a political struggle against the status quo. I'll say once again that it does feel like it's happening again to some degree, and it would be great to see more of that collaboration going forward.

Thank you for sharing that. And thanks so much Michael for taking the time to speak with me today!

Michael

has been living in squats in London since 2011 and is still doing so. He's an advocate of finding new ways of organising ourselves, socially and technologically. He lives and works within the sphere of homelessness, and sees it as part of a bigger struggle against the prevailing political and economic environment.

Cults Happen

IAN HAWORTH

... make sure they don't happen to you. In this final article, founder of the Cult Information Centre, Ian Haworth, shares his knowledge on how cults exercise control, what the warning signs are, and what it takes to leave a cult.

Idealism, that provokes a person with a deep desire to make the world a better place, can lead them through a variety of open doors into differing communities. Some of those doors then slam shut psychologically, after the person has entered. These communities operate against the individual member's interests and wellbeing and are known as cults.

In the UK, I suggest there are up to a thousand cults in operation and this is a conservative estimate. Some cults operate communes and some of those give the appearance of running intentional communities of free thinking people, who have all joined of their own free will. People need to be alert and far more discerning before assuming a communal group is a safe place to be.

Cults radicalise people to deprive them of their assets, control their relationships and psychologically force them to work for the cult in a relatively new form of slavery. Why is that not illegal? Sadly, it is happening throughout the UK. It is not yet illegal, as the law has not yet caught up with this phenomenon. As a consequence, there is no protection for UK citizens from tactics used by groups that psychologically coerce them to the point of full control of an individual's life. Laws relating to slavery do not apply in this context because people are not being physically held, but psychologically held instead.

Many people believe that since they have no intention of 'joining' a cult, they are safe. Think again. No one joins a cult. Instead, they are recruited. However, some people also feel that they could not be recruited because they are too intelligent and not easily led. This is a popular myth that suggests that people, who become cult members, must be lacking in some way. The reverse is true, so much so that the easiest people to recruit and indoctrinate into cult involvement are people with healthy minds and average or above average intelligence. In fact, it appears that the hardest people to recruit into a cult are the very seriously mentally ill. It's just the opposite of what society usually imagines.

For many years another myth has been promoted that suggests that cults only recruit young people, however the word 'young' might be defined. It isn't true and never has been. Cults recruit people of all ages from sixteen to ninety and older, if they live long enough. At the point of recruitment, cult members may have been students, teachers, lawyers, doctors, civil servants, politicians, mental health workers and journalists along with people from every other profession. They recruit people from all walks of life.

Considering the awful things that are done to cult members, perhaps we shouldn't be surprised that cult leaders appear to be people without a conscience and are motivated by greed, power over others, or even a desire for world domination. It is therefore not surprising that critics of cults sometimes describe these cult leaders as psychopaths or sociopaths. Cult leaders are not the only people viewed in this way. When we look at the causes for war in different parts of the world, we often see the same motives at play in those leaders of warring factions.

It is important to remember that taking the wrong path and ending up in a cult can be devastating for the individual and their family. Cult members are always abused psychologically and can be abused financially, sexually and physically. As a consequence, cult members have sometimes lost their jobs, their marriages and other relationships. Some have lost their lives! It is therefore important to thoroughly analyse any new association with a group, whether or not it operates as a commune.

Warning signs

How can you tell if someone you know may have been recruited into a cult? What are the signs to look for? There are two main changes. One is a change of personality. A cult member will be forced psychologically to adopt a different personality to the one they exhibited prior to involvement. Their new personality will now be more or less the same as that of every other member of the cult. It is as though they, the new recruit, have become a clone of the group. This change of personality is referred to as 'Snapping' and was first outlined in detail in their book (of the same name), by Conway and Siegelman, 1978.

With all of the above in mind, what then does one look for in a commune that may suggest problems ahead? If a group or commune is run as a cult, there are quite a few warning signs for people once they know what to look for. One issue is whether or not you are allowed to visit the community and wander around talking to whomever you please. If instead, it is all controlled by a guide, who may be there to give you only one perspective, then that may just be nothing more than a self-promotional exercise, so you'll have less chance to see and hear the reality. In other words, what you see is not what you get in a cult. A cult will only give you a public relations look at its activities, through rose tinted glasses.

Another clue is when the group is claiming that you will not be paid for work done, but instead you'll be given a roof over your head and food and clothing. That may sound very attractive at first, especially if initially you have little in the way of funds. However, the longer you are in the group, the longer you will remain in a financially impoverished condition. If, at some point in the future, you realise that all is not what you thought it would be, or as it was promised, it may be difficult to leave and start a new life elsewhere, because of your lack of funds, especially if you have lived there for a few years. One may therefore ask oneself, "Do I get paid for the jobs I do in the commune? If not, who profits from my work?"

As you might imagine, if you ask a cult leader where the money goes, you may not receive a reliable answer. It is common for cult leaders to claim that funds raised in a cult go to feed the hungry, clothe the poor, or to some other worthy cause, when in fact the profits go directly or indirectly into cult leaders' pockets. In fact many cult leaders have access to bank accounts holding millions. They then can and often do hire the best lawyers to try to silence critics, so it's always important to know, in advance of association with a group, where the money is going and who controls the funds.

Psychological control

However, the above items aren't major issues in terms of psychological coercion, so what should one look for in terms of group techniques that may start to break you down and control you?

Most people imagine that if a person can be controlled, the psychologically coercive methods used by a group must be easy to spot and probably take a long time to bring about full control. Actually, I would argue that many cults are likely to be able to completely control the average person within just three or four days. That's all the time they actually need.

One mind control method frequently used by cults is hypnosis. In some groups hypnosis is disguised as a breakthrough form of 'meditation,' or it may be called a special 'process,' or perhaps 'going within.' There are many terms used to avoid describing it accurately as hypnosis. As a consequence, if a commune has daily 'meditation' times, one needs to know what the word meditation means in that particular group. If it means sitting down and closing one's eyes whilst a leader is speaking to the group in highs and lows and in a repetitive fashion for prolonged periods, perhaps this is a trance-inducing activity. In a hypnotic trance critics argue that you can be programmed to do anything that a group and its leader requires. It also seems that the more this happens, the quicker one goes into a trance state and the deeper too. There are two other very common activities to bring about a trance state in a potential cult member. One is chanting a mantra scores or hundreds of times. The other is staring at an object for a prolonged period of time. Hypnosis and other trance-inducing methods are frequently employed in the world of cults.

Meditation may even be advertised as a method to reduce crime and violence in the world and the group may take credit for areas in the country where law-breaking is in decline. It is sometimes promoted as a way to look younger, to study more effectively, or if you are a nurse to be able to improve your bedside manner. On the other hand, if you are or were a jour-

nalist, artist, teacher, or politician, the cult may claim
that the meditation will make you more creative. In
other words, they talk to you about you, find out your
interests and passions and tell you anything you would
like to hear in favour of the trance inducing process,
where your critical faculties will be overruled.

If the group emphasises that members need less than
normal amounts of sleep, this can help to fatigue people
and make them less able to engage in clear judgement
but instead make them more compliant. It is frequently
used by cults to manipulate their members. In addition, the food in some cults is modified to give one
less nutrients than one's body needs. That also helps
to break the person down and cause them to be less
alert and less critically able.

Some groups will have a special course for new people.
Classes may be conducted in some kind of structure
with walls, so that daylight can be shut out. When
the course takes place in a room with no windows,
or where the windows are covered with blackout
curtaining (or equivalent), course participants will
not be able to guess the time of day by judging from
the daylight conditions outside. Linked with this, the
group may also request that watches are not worn,
supposedly so that time isn't a distraction. However,
in reality, it is done so that new people will not know
what time of day it is. By then giving them less food
and/or eating at peculiar times of day, people on the
course will have their circadian rhythms broken, thus
leaving them more vulnerable to further manipulation
and suggestion.

Although it is not the most common, verbal abuse is
yet another method sometimes used by a cult, to try
to silence a critic or questioner. In a cult lecture, if
someone breaks the rules and starts asking questions,
when they are not supposed to do so, or they break
some other rule, the session leader may well verbally
abuse them in some way, in front of the rest of the
class. This will be an attempt to embarrass them and
stop them from asking additional questions. It may
also inhibit others present from doing so.

Another common technique is to have all the other
members of the group work against you through group
pressure, in order to make the new person conform.
However, one needs to keep in mind that the group's
cult members are innocent victims, but they become
victimisers too, because they automatically obey the

leader's commands. They are likely to be instructed to speak positively about the group and how they have benefitted by being in the commune. Similarly, they will also be led to speak negatively about anything critical said about the group by a new potential recruit or outside source. Because cult members are victims and under the control of the group, they are unable to think for themselves, so they are sincere. However, sincerity can often be misunderstood and to some people it may suggest honesty or reliability, but surely one can be sincere and yet both sincerely in trouble and sincerely wrong.

In a typical cult it is usual for the group to use 'love bombing' as a technique to manipulate the unsuspecting. New people will appear to be showered with love and warmth. However, if the receiver of this 'affection' does not tow the party line, or starts to ask awkward questions, the love will usually be turned off and the person may well be shunned until he or she conforms. It is therefore easy to see that this is not legitimate or unconditional love. Instead, it is conditional love.

Removal of privacy is another technique of mind control that is frequently used by cults. Instead of being given your own space and free time to occupy that space, the workload and other activities will be high and you will have to share space with others when working, eating and sleeping. This allows all the cult members to monitor each other and report anyone who is not operating in line with the orders of the leader or rules within the group, so they can be challenged and caused to 'reform'.

By using the psychologically coercive technique of rejecting old values, most cult groups will heavily criticise the rest of the world, suggesting their group is the only one with the answer, or it is the only one that has discovered 'the way forward'. The cult group members now comprise the elite on this earth. As a consequence, cult members are programmed to understand that being above others in the world, they don't need help, but everyone else does. This helps to further isolate them from society and the reality of what is happening to them.

In some cases a cult group will require a particular way of dressing. This may or may not be different from the traditional way of dressing in that part of a country or the world. If the dress code does not appear to be different from that of others outside of the group, it will mean that all are conforming to a small change that is still there, even if it is not obvious. An example of this might be something as simple as men in the group not being allowed to wear ties. By dressing in this manner, all the cult members will be visually supporting each other's need to conform.

What could be wrong with asking questions? Well, cult groups don't seem to like them. Some groups even have a 'no questions' policy, at least until a break is called. However, when the intermission starts, often after many hours of listening to lectures, people rush to the loo instead of questioning. Then because the breaks are so short, by the time they return to the class, the next session is already starting, so there is then no time for their question(s) to be asked. Other people just forget their questions, especially after so much time has elapsed.

The more questions you find you can ask by phone, by email or in person, the less likely the group's members are to give clear answers. If instead, you get a response along the lines of "Come live with us for a while and you'll see what it's like". I would suggest you stay away! Cult methods of psychological coercion work, even if you know these techniques are going to be used against you! One might compare this with knowing that a particular gas is poisonous, but if you allow yourself to inhale it, it will still harm you. Knowledge of a cult being a cult does not stop its mind control methods working on you. So, trying to experience life in a potential cult is far from being an appropriate way to assess the safety of a group.

Again, a common technique used against people in a cult environment, is confession. This may be introduced in a time of 'sharing,' where people are encouraged to tell everyone present bad things that they had done or that have been done to them. Firstly, this creates a bonding feeling with all present, who you perceive as 'friends and allies,' at the time. Secondly, it is information of a sensitive nature that may well be documented and used to keep you quiet in the future, if you escape the group and want to expose the organisation, as a cult, to the wider world.

Isolation is used by many cults too. This is particularly easy to achieve in a rural commune. The further away you are from family, friends, a library, access to the internet and other reasonable sources of information, the less likely you are to find information exposing a cult for the serious problem it represents. So isolation comes in two forms. There is sometimes isolation that is achieved geographically, when a cult is based in the middle of nowhere. However, there may also be isolation from access to the real world, via the removal of a computer, tablet or mobile phone, for supposed safe keeping or to 'stop you being interrupted.'

It is not unusual for a cult to use a system of 'controlled approval'. One may be praised for doing or saying something one day, but not another day, when one may instead be disciplined in some way. This helps to maintain vulnerability and confusion in the new potential recruit, by alternately rewarding and punishing similar actions.

Ex-cult members, who have escaped from cults, also talk about being indoctrinated with fear. It could be fear about the destiny of the world, or fear of a loss of salvation, fear of some imaginary 'enemy' being on the doorstep. So fear is another weapon in the armoury of a cult leader that is used to control people.

Many cult-related communes change the relationships that people normally enjoy. They sometimes forbid intimate relationships all together, even between married couples. Other groups put different restrictions on the types of relationships that are allowed to take place. By controlling personal relationships, normal expressions of love have less chance of interfering with the psychological control implemented by the group and its leader on the membership.

Some cults claim to be able to take people off drugs. So, one might wonder if that is perhaps a good thing. For me, if it is proved to be true and not just typical cult propaganda, then I would suggest that what it proves is that psychological coercion is more powerful than drug addiction. This in turn means that the person is still in very serious trouble and under control, but a type of control related to a group rather than a specific drug. In some ways, the new control/addiction can therefore be viewed as being worse than drug addiction.

Leaving a cult

Usually, cults recruit people with the intention of keeping them for life. Is it possible for a person to 'snap' back to reality and walk away? Yes, it is. Is it likely to happen? It may, but it may be after one year, five years, twenty-five years, fifty years and it may never happen. There is no guarantee that any cult recruit will escape the psychological clutches of a cult at some point in the future.

So, what can you do if you hear that a close friend or family member has become involved in a cult? You need to proceed very carefully and read up on the general phenomenon as well as the specific group. It is usually best to also consult people specialising in cults. Once armed with useful and accurate information from a variety of sources, one can try to engage the cult victim in dialogue or correspondence. However, it is important to be careful to not let the cult member know you have learned it is a cult, but instead to ask questions in a very loving and gentle way about their new association. Also, you need to keep in mind that the cult member now has limited ability to use logic, so please don't think that what seems obvious to you will be obvious to them. This is a very difficult procedure, with no guarantees of success, but there is also no reason why you cannot win back their freedom, even if it takes years.

Whether it is after five weeks or fifty years of involvement, if a person does escape from a cult, it will usually take them a year or more of suffering very painful symptoms of withdrawal, before they fully recover. When they have fully recovered, they will at last have returned to their original personality and regained their ability to think clearly and to critically evaluate.

For some people, the symptoms of withdrawal include hallucinations and delusions. Most ex-cult members will suffer from insomnia and amnesia. Some will also suffer from suicidal tendencies, abnormal weight gain or loss and many others with general confusion about who to trust and what to do next with one's life. Many ex-cult members will find it difficult to concentrate for a long time. Reading more than two or three paragraphs of the printed word can be very difficult to do as one tries to recover from a cult experience. It is a tough time for all who are fortunate enough to break away from a cult. During the withdrawal, people need help and support, but sadly, the average mental health professional does not seem to understand the phenomenon, so with the best intentions can even sometimes make things worse.

As you can see, it is so important to recognise that some groups of people living communally are a serious threat to the welfare of others they try to ensnare. Therefore, there is a great need to vet new associations with groups, as thoroughly as one can, before taking that first step in the direction of a possible cult. To aid in one's checking of a group ahead of possibly visiting it, why not look on the internet for critical information. A good way to do so is to put the name of the group into a search engine, followed by words like cult, harm, damage and recovery, to see what stories may surface. In addition, one can always contact people and organisations specialising in cults... Most have a great deal of information at their fingertips to share with the public.

© **Ian Haworth 2023**

Ian Haworth

has been a specialist in cults for 44 years. He is the founder of the Cult Information Centre and was the co-founder of two organisations in Canada and the USA. Over the years, he has given over 1,000 lectures to schools, colleges, universities, professional associations, companies and community groups. He is the author of the booklet *Cults: A Practical Guide* and has spoken to thousands of families with loved ones in cults and assisted many hundreds of ex-cult members in their recovery. Along with speaking to police, law firms, the media, social agencies, religious institutions, educators, mental health professionals and corporations Ian has also been an expert witness in cult-related civil and criminal trials in both Canada and the UK.

Resources

The following is a select list/contact details of recent publications and other reports related to urban communal living

Books

■ ADVISORY SERVICE FOR SQUATTERS. *The Squatters Handbook – 14th Edition.* ASS; (2016) ISBN: 978-0950776972

■ BIBBY, A. *These Houses Are Ours – Co-operative and community housing alternatives 1870-1919.* Gritstone Publishing Co-Operative; (2023) ISBN: 978-1913625085

Reviewed by Chris Coates

Hidden away in the suburban sprawl on the east side of Leicester, Humberstone Garden Village is a somewhat unique housing scheme. Unique – not for just being an early example of a garden suburb development predating both Letchworth & Hampstead , nor for reaching its centenary largely with its original structure intact, but for being the only garden village ever to be be built by the members of a workers co-operative. I know about it because my grandfather knew people who lived there and was a regular visitor. But I doubt many people in Leicester even know it exists. Let alone that there were dozens of such co-partnership schemes around the country.

Andrew Bibby in his new book These Houses Are Ours brings these early 'Community Led Housing' schemes out of obscurity and shines a light on the struggles and achievements of people trying to provide decent homes for themselves at the turn of the twentieth century. There are stories of schemes across the country from the Welsh Valleys to Suffolk and from Brighton to Stirling and what feels like almost every other place in between. Set up sometimes by local political activists, sometimes by well meaning philanthropists and in some cases, as in the Leicester scheme, by workers themselves. Many of the people involved were also part of the wider thriving co-operative movement at the time. A few of the 150 schemes never made it off the drawing board, others went on to build getting on for 10,000 houses before the movement began to run out of steam after WW1. Some have since morphed into desirable suburbs, but a few have continued to honour the original aim to provide decent affordable housing for ordinary people.

Reading the trials and tribulations of trying to get finance, find land and get building contractors, you could be forgiven for thinking you are reading about the problems faced by a community land trust or cohousing project today. A point Bibby makes himself in the book "What is extraordinary is how similar what com-

munity land trusts are doing today is to what was being done 100 years ago...We have the same desires, the same issues and the same dilemmas..."

While doing research for Utopia Britannica I walked in my grandfather's footsteps, so to speak, around the streets of the Humberstone garden village and was stopped by an elderly resident who wanted to know "Was I from the electricity board?". When I told her I was interested in the history of the place and that my grandfather had been a regular visitor in its early days she invited me in for a cup of tea and told me her and her late husband's story of how they came to live there and what a lovely place it had been – and really still was when she thought about it.

"I hope that those involved in co-operative housing, co-housing or community land trusts can get to know their history and that they're not starting from scratch," Andrew Bibby.

CHRISTIAN, D.L. *Creating a Life Together: Practical Tools to Grow Ecovillages and Intentional Communities.* New Society Publishers; (2003) ISBN: 978-0-86571-471-7

CLEAVER, N. and FREARSON, A. *All Together Now: The co-living and co-working revolution.* RIBA Publishing; (2021) ISBN: 978-1859468982

DELZ, S.; HEHL, R.; and VENTURA, P. *Housing the Co-op – A Micropolitical Manifesto.* Ruby Press; (2020) ISBN: 978-3944074313

Housing the Co-op shows how co-operative housing construction and forms of self-determined building production offer effective solutions to the global housing crisis. The manifesto and accompanying essays with case studies from Africa, Asia, Europe, and the Americas make a claim that by combining micro-political actions and co-operative practices we can move closer to a systemic change for a more sustainable and equitable future. A glossary of co-operative housing explains important terms.

HERTZBERG, M, SMITH, R and WESTPHA, R. *A Consensus Handbook: Co-operative decision-making for activists, co-ops and communities.* Seeds for Change Lancaster Co-operative (2013) ISBN: 978-0957587106

HOGGARTH, J. *The Single Mum's Mansion.* Arla; (2018) ISBN: 978-1-788548625

LUDWIG, M. *Together Resilient: Building Community in an Age of Climate Disruption.* Fellowship for Intentional Community; (2017) ISBN: 978-0971826472

■ MONBIOT, G. *Out of the Wreckage: A New Politics for an Age of Crisis.* Verso (2018) ISBN: 978-1786632890

> George Monbiot makes the case for four pillars of society: business, state, home and commons. It's a great place to start to reimagine how the social contract might be reconstructed to ensure a viable future which embraces all humanity and reinvents political life beyond entrenched bipartisanship, and the false dichotomy of individualism and pluralism.

■ RAU, T and KOCH-GONZALEZ, J. *Many Voices One Song: Shared power with Sociocracy.* Institute for Peaceable Communities (2018) ISBN-13: 978-1949183009

■ RUSSELL, C and McKNIGHT, J. *The Connected Community: Discovering the Health, Wealth, and Power of Neighbourhoods.* Berrett-Koehler (2022) ISBN-13: 978-15230025285

■ SKINNER, M. *Living Together.* Footnote Press; (2022) ISBN: 978-1-04440032

Websites

■ Advisory Service for Squatters
www.network23.org/ass

■ London Renters Union
www.londonrentersunion.org

■ Coliving.com
www.coliving.com

■ Radical Routes
www.radicalroutes.org.uk

■ Confederation of Co-operative Housing
www.cch.coop

■ Spare Room
www.spareroom.co.uk

■ Co-operatives UK
www.uk.coop

■ UK Cohousing Network
www.cohousing.org.uk

■ Foundation for Intentional Community
www.ic.org

■ Sociocracy for All
www.sociocracyforall.org

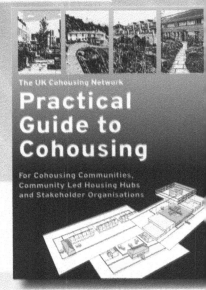

Historical Books from D&D

An Adventure Shared
Rachel Rowlands
198 pp £12, ISBN: 978-0-9545757-6-2

The story of the first Quaker
Community at Bamford.

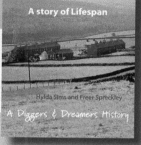

Commune on the Moors
Freer Spreckley and Hylda Sims
200 pp £12, ISBN: 978-0-9545757-8-6

A history of the Lifespan Community –
high up in the Pennines.

Anatomy of a Commune
Dave Treanor et al (eds)
358 pp £12, ISBN: 978-0-9545757-9-3

Multiple perspectives on the first 15
years of Laurieston Hall Community.

A Life in Common
Chris Coates
198 pp £12, ISBN: 978-1-8384725-0-4

Recollections of People in Common –
from Burnley to Altham Corn Mill.

Utopia Britannica
Chris Coates
312 pp £16.50, 978-0-9514945-8-5

British utopian experiments from 1325 to 1945.

Communes Britannica
Chris Coates
520 pp £25, ISBN: 978-0-9514945-9-2

Communal living in Britain from 1939 to 2000.

Overview

*Here's a selection of UK urban intentional communities
as they existed at the time of publication*

	postcode	year started	number of adults	number of children	daily communal m...
151 Housing Co-operative	NE4 5PE	1989			
Argyle Street Housing Co-operative	CB1 3LU	1981	85	7	■
Bath Street Housing Co-op	EH15 1EZ	1984	4		■
Blackcurrent	NN1 4JQ	1989	7		■
Brambles Housing Co-op	S3 9EH	1992	7		■
Cambridge Cohousing Marmalade Lane	CB4 2ZE	2019	70	40	■
Cohousing Bristol	BS3 5ES	2001	11		■
Cornerstone Housing Co-operative	LS7 3HB	1993	16		■
Deptford Housing Co-operative	SE8 4LY	1978	80		
Dragonfly	OX4 3NR	2000			
Dragons Co-op	SY10 0JW	2015	3		
Edinburgh Student Housing Co-op	EH10 4HR	2014	106		
Firelight Housing Co-op	LS6 2JG				
Fireside Housing Co-op	S3 9DN	1996	10	3	■
Fruit Corner	BS6 5BU	2000	15	1	■
Giffard Park Housing Co-op	MK14 5PA	1984			
Golem Housing Co-operative	SA1 6AB	2012	12	1	■
Green Wood Housing Co-operative	LS8 4DW	2019			■
Guiseppe Conlon House	N4 1BG	2010	5		■
Gung Ho Housing Co-op	B29 7PX	2009	5		■
Hamwic Housing Co-op	SO17 1WF		50		
Hargrave Road Community	N19 5SJ	1987	12		■
LILAC	LS5 3AG	2008	33	12	■
Mornington Grove Community	E3 4NS	1982	11		■
Nutclough Housing Co-op	HX7 8HA	2002	7		■
Oakfield Road Community	N4 4LB	2000	5		■
Oakleigh	S4 7AG	2000	8		■
Pendragon House	BA6 8AQ	2013	9	6	
Quaggy Housing Co-op	SE14 6HW	2020	5		
Rainbow Housing Co-operative	MK13 0DW	1977	31	6	
Redcurrant Housing Co-op	G5 0HY	2017	6		■
Rose Howey Housing Co-operative	L8 3TD	2012	12	9	
Sanford Housing Co-operative	SE14 6NB	1973	119		
Scraptoft Housing Co-op	LE5 2FE	2015	5		■
Share Instead	S6 4WA	2012	5		■
Skylark Housing Co-op	BN2 4LR	2009	6		■
The Drive Housing Co-op	E17 3BW	2010	11		
The Nevill Community	N16 8SL	1991			■
Torch Housing Co-op	B18 5NH	1994	9		■
Wellhouse Community	LN7 6TX	2013	4	1	■
West End Housing Co-operative	NE4 5NL	1979	17	1	

.